I0447461

United States
Department of
Agriculture

Forest Service

FS-978

July 2011

Watershed Condition Classification Technical Guide

"Ultimately, our success at the Forest Service will be measured in terms of watershed health on those 193 million acres of national forests and grasslands."

Tom Tidwell
Chief, Forest Service
April 29, 2010

Primary Authors

John P. Potyondy
Program Manager and Hydrologist
Stream Systems Technology Center
Watershed, Fish, Wildlife, Air, and Rare Plants Staff
Washington Office

Theodore W. Geier
Regional Hydrologist
Eastern Region

Cover photo: *Pisgah National Forest by Jack Holcomb.*

Contributors

Watershed Condition Advisory Team Members (October 2010)

John Potyondy	Washington Office (WO), Watershed, Fish, Wildlife, Air and Rare Plants (WFWARP), Stream Systems Technology Center
Ted Geier	Eastern Region (R-9), Regional Office, Regional Hydrologist
Penny Luehring	WO, WFWARP, Watershed Improvement Program Leader
Mark Hudy	WO, WFWARP, Fish and Aquatic Ecology Unit (FAEU)
Brett Roper	WO, WFWARP, FAEU
Ron Dunlap	WO, WFWARP, Assistant Director, Watershed, Fish, and Air (retired)
Tom Doane	Eastern Region (R-9), Deputy Director, Air, Water, Lands, Soils, Minerals and Environmental Engineering/Services
Greg Kujawa	WO, Forest Management
Paul T. Anderson	WO, Engineering
Jaelith Hall-Rivera	WO, Fire and Aviation Management
Jim Keys	WO, Ecosystem Management Coordination
Michael Ielmini	WO, Invasive Species Program
Ann Acheson	WO, WFWARP Air Program
Ray Thompson	WO, Program and Budget
Bob Davis	Southwestern Region (R-3), Regional Director's Representative
Sharon Friedman	Rocky Mountain Region (R-2), Strategic Planning Director
Karl Dalla Rosa	WO, State and Private Forestry (Forest Stewardship Program)
Thomas Brown	Rocky Mountain Research Station
Vacant	WO, Rangeland Management
Vacant	WO, Environmental Sciences Research

Major Contributors to Indicator Rule Sets Development

Water Quality	John Potyondy, Ted Geier, Cindy Huber
Water Quantity	John Potyondy, Ted Geier
Aquatic Habitat	Mark Hudy, Brett Roper, John Potyondy
Aquatic Biota	Mark Hudy, Brett Roper

Riparian/Wetland Vegetation	Penny Luehring
Roads and Trails	Paul T. Anderson
Soils	Penny Luehring, Cindy Huber
Fire Regime or Wildfire	Jaelith Hall-Rivera, Penny Luehring
Forest Cover	Greg Kujawa
Rangeland Vegetation	Charles Quimby
Terrestrial Invasive Species	Michael Ielmini
Forest Health	Borys Tkacz, Cindy Huber

Contents

Introduction

The U.S. Department of Agriculture (USDA) Strategic Plan for fiscal year (FY) 2010–2015 targets the restoration of watershed and forest health as a core management objective of the national forests and grasslands. To achieve this goal, the Forest Service, an agency of USDA, is directed to restore degraded watersheds by strategically focusing investments in watershed improvement projects and conservation practices at landscape and watershed scales.

In a 2006 review of the Forest Service Watershed Program, the Office of Management and Budget (OMB) concluded that the Forest Service lacks a nationally consistent approach to prioritize watersheds for improvement (OMB 2006). The OMB also noted that the current Forest Service direction in the Forest Service Manual (FSM) 2521 for tracking watershed condition class is vague, open to varied interpretation, and insufficient to consistently evaluate watershed condition or track how condition changes over time. To address these issues, the Forest Service formed the National Watershed Condition Team and tasked it with developing a nationally consistent, science-based approach to classify the condition of all National Forest System (NFS) watersheds and to develop outcome-based performance measures for watershed restoration. The team evaluated alternative approaches for classifying watersheds (USDA Forest Service 2007) and developed the watershed condition classification (WCC) system described in this technical guide.

The team designed the WCC system to—

- Classify the condition of all NFS watersheds.

- Be quantitative to the extent feasible.

- Rely on Geographic Information System (GIS) technology.

- Be cost effective.

- Be implementable within existing budgets.

- Include resource areas and activities that have a significant influence on watershed condition.

National forests are required to revise the classification on an annual basis. We will use change in watershed condition class as an outcome-based performance measure of progress toward improving watershed condition on NFS lands. In order to demonstrate improvement in condition class, we need to track activities at the smallest feasible watershed unit, the 6th-level hydrologic unit (typically 10,000 to 40,000 acres in size).

The WCC system is a national forest-based, reconnaissance-level evaluation of watershed condition achievable within existing budgets and staffing levels that can be aggregated for a national assessment of watershed condition. The WCC system offers a systematic, flexible means of classifying watersheds based on a core set of national watershed condition indicators. The system relies on professional judgment exercised by forest interdisciplinary (ID) teams, GIS data, and national databases to the extent they are available, and on written rule sets and criteria for indicators that describe the three watershed condition classes (functioning properly, functioning at risk, and impaired function). The WCC system relies on Washington Office and regional office oversight for flexible and consistent application among national forests. The WCC system is a first approximation of watershed condition, and we will revise and refine it over time. The expectation is that we will improve and refine individual resource indicators and that we will develop databases and map products to assist with future classifications. The WCC information will be incorporated into the watershed condition framework, which will ultimately be employed to establish priorities, evaluate program performance, and communicate watershed restoration successes to interested stakeholders and Congress.

Objectives of This Guide

The watershed condition goal of the Forest Service is "to protect National Forest System watersheds by implementing practices designed to maintain or improve watershed condition, which is the foundation for sustaining ecosystems and the production of renewable natural resources, values, and benefits" (FSM 2520). U.S. Secretary of Agriculture Tom Vilsack reemphasized this policy in his "Vision for the Forest Service" when he stated that achieving restoration of watershed and forest health would be the primary management objective of the Forest Service (USDA 2010). This *Watershed Condition Classification Technical Guide* helps to implement this policy objective by—

1. Establishing a systematic process for determining watershed condition class that all national forests can apply consistently.

2. Improving Forest Service reporting and tracking of watershed condition.

3. Strengthening the effectiveness of the Forest Service to maintain and restore the productivity and resilience of watersheds and their associated aquatic systems on NFS lands.

Defining Watershed Condition

Watershed condition is the state of the physical and biological characteristics and processes within a watershed that affect the hydrologic and soil functions supporting aquatic ecosystems. Watershed condition reflects a range of variability from natural pristine (functioning properly) to degraded (severely altered state or impaired). Watersheds that are functioning properly have terrestrial, riparian, and aquatic ecosystems that capture, store, and release water, sediment, wood, and nutrients within their range of natural variability for these processes. When watersheds are functioning properly, they create and sustain functional terrestrial, riparian, aquatic, and wetland habitats that are capable of supporting diverse populations of native aquatic- and riparian-dependent species. In general, the greater the departure from the natural pristine state, the more impaired the watershed condition is likely to be. Watersheds that are functioning properly are commonly referred to as healthy watersheds.

Watersheds that are functioning properly have five important characteristics (Williams et al. 1997):

1. They provide for high biotic integrity, which includes habitats that support adaptive animal and plant communities that reflect natural processes.

2. They are resilient and recover rapidly from natural and human disturbances.

3. They exhibit a high degree of connectivity longitudinally along the stream, laterally across the floodplain and valley bottom, and vertically between surface and subsurface flows.

4. They provide important ecosystem services, such as high-quality water, the recharge of streams and aquifers, the maintenance of riparian communities, and the moderation of climate variability and change.

5. They maintain long-term soil productivity.

Watershed condition classification is the process of describing watershed condition in terms of discrete categories (or classes) that reflect the level of watershed health or integrity. In our usage, we consider watershed health and integrity are conceptually the same (Regier 1993): watersheds with high integrity are in an unimpaired condition in which ecosystems show little or no influence from human actions (Lackey 2001).

The FSM uses three classes to describe watershed condition (USDA Forest Service 2004, FSM 2521.1).

1. Class 1 watersheds exhibit high geomorphic, hydrologic, and biotic integrity relative to their natural potential condition.

2. Class 2 watersheds exhibit moderate geomorphic, hydrologic, and biotic integrity relative to their natural potential condition.

3. Class 3 watersheds exhibit low geomorphic, hydrologic, and biotic integrity relative to their natural potential condition.

The FSM classification defines watershed condition in terms of "geomorphic, hydrologic and biotic integrity" relative to "potential natural condition." In this context, integrity relates directly to functionality. We define geomorphic functionality or integrity in terms of attributes such as slope stability, soil erosion, channel morphology, and other upslope, riparian, and aquatic habitat characteristics. Hydrologic functionality or integrity relates primarily to flow, sediment, and water-quality attributes. Biological functionality or integrity is defined by the characteristics that influence the diversity and abundance of aquatic species, terrestrial vegetation, and soil productivity. In each case, integrity is evaluated in the context of the natural disturbance regime, geoclimatic setting, and other important factors within the context of a watershed. The definition encompasses both aquatic and terrestrial components because water quality and aquatic habitat are inseparably related to the integrity and, therefore, the functionality of upland and riparian areas within a watershed.

Within this context, the three watershed condition classes are directly related to the degree or level of watershed functionality or integrity:

1. Class 1 = Functioning Properly.

2. Class 2 = Functioning at Risk.

3. Class 3 = Impaired Function.

In this guide, we characterize a watershed in good condition as one that is functioning in a manner similar to natural wildland conditions (Karr and Chu 1999, Lackey 2001). A watershed is considered to be functioning properly if the physical attributes are adequate to maintain or improve biological integrity. This consideration implies that a Class 1 watershed that is functioning properly has minimal undesirable human impact on its natural, physical, or biological processes, and it is resilient and able to recover to the desired condition when disturbed by large natural disturbances or land management activities (Yount and Neimi 1990). By contrast, a Class 3 watershed has impaired function because some physical, hydrological, or biological threshold has been exceeded. Substantial changes to the factors that caused the degraded state are commonly needed to return the watershed to a properly functioning condition.

Defining specific classes for watershed condition is subjective and problematic for several reasons. First, watershed condition is not directly observable (Suter 1993). In nature, no distinct lines separate watersheds that are functioning properly from impaired watersheds, and, therefore, every classification scheme is arbitrary to some extent. Second, watershed condition is a mental construct that has numerous definitions and interpretations in the scientific literature (Lackey 2001). Third, the attributes that reflect the state of a watershed are continually changing because of natural disturbances (e.g., wildfire, landslides, floods, insects, and disease), natural variability of ecological processes (e.g., flows and cycles of energy, nutrients, and water), climate variability and change, and human modifications.

Watershed Condition and Ecological Restoration

The most effective way to approach complex ecological issues is to consider them at the watershed level, where the fundamental connection among all components of the landscape is the network of streams that define the basin (Heller 2004, National Research Council 1999, Newbold 2002, Ogg and Keith 2002, Reid et al. 1996, Sedell et al. 2000, Smith et al. 2005, Williams et al. 1997). Watersheds are also readily recognized by local communities and resonate with much of the public as a logical way to address resource management issues. Watersheds are easily identified on maps and on the ground, and their boundaries do not change much over time (Reid et al. 1996).

Watersheds are integral parts of broader ecosystems, and we can view and evaluate them at a variety of spatial scales. Because watersheds are spatially located landscape features

that have been uniformly mapped for the entire United States at multiple scales, they are ideal for tracking watershed improvement accomplishments both in terms of outputs (acres treated on the ground) and outcomes (improvement in watershed condition class). Reporting accomplishments and outcomes by each watershed's unique hydrologic unit code (HUC) avoids double counting. The WCC system analyzes the effect of all activities within a watershed; therefore, the system provides an ideal mechanism for interpreting the cumulative effect over time of a multitude of management actions on hydrologic and soil function. Finally, many hydrologic and aquatic restoration issues can be properly addressed only within the confines of watershed boundaries. Watersheds provide a basis for developing restoration plans and priorities that can treat a multitude of resource problems in a structured, comprehensive manner.

Many terrestrial ecological restoration issues, however, are poorly addressed in a watershed context. Ecological restoration issues dealing with vegetation and wildlife species composition, structure, pattern, and diversity may not affect hydrologic and soil functions and are best evaluated using ecological stratifications such as those depicted in the map, Bailey's Ecoregions and Subregions of the United States, Puerto Rico, and the U.S. Virgin Islands (Bailey 1995). Consequently, we view watershed condition, watershed health, and watershed restoration as a subset of ecological condition, ecological health, and ecological restoration.

In summary, ecological restoration focuses on the composition, structure, pattern, and ecological processes necessary to make terrestrial and aquatic ecosystems sustainable, resilient, and healthy under current and future conditions. This includes watershed condition and health. Watershed condition assessment places specific emphasis on the physical and biological characteristics and processes affecting hydrologic and soil functions that support aquatic ecosystems. Therefore, in this WCC system, primary emphasis is placed on indicators that directly or indirectly affect soil and hydrologic functions and associated riparian and aquatic ecosystems.

Watershed Condition Indicators

The WCC system described in this technical guide uses 12 indicators composed of attributes related to watershed processes. The indicators and their attributes are surrogate variables representing the underlying ecological functions and processes that affect soil and hydrologic function. For most of the indicators, the Forest Service can take direct action, or cause others to take action, which contributes to maintaining or improving watershed condition. This structure provides for a direct linkage between the classification system and management or improvement activities the Forest Service conducts on the ground. Because of this linkage, when a sufficient number of properly designed and implemented restoration and/or management actions occur within a watershed, we can express the outcome as a change in condition class and use the resulting change in condition class for performance accountability purposes. Management activities that affect the watershed condition class are not limited to soil and water improvement activities; they include a broad array of resource program areas: hazardous fuel treatments, invasive species eradication, abandoned mine restoration, riparian area treatments, aquatic organism passage improvement, road maintenance and obliteration, and others. To change a watershed condition class will, in most cases, require changes within a watershed that are significant in their scope and include treatments from multiple resource areas. Sound management or improving management practices can often be as effective as implementing restoration projects and must not be overlooked. To demonstrate improvement in condition class, we will need to track activities at the smallest feasible watershed unit, the 6th-level HUC (typically, 10,000 to 40,000 acres).[1]

The WCC system consists of 12 watershed condition indicators:

1. Water Quality
2. Water Quantity
3. Aquatic Habitat
4. Aquatic Biota
5. Riparian/Wetland Vegetation
6. Roads and Trails
7. Soils
8. Fire Regime or Wildfire
9. Forest Cover
10. Rangeland Vegetation
11. Terrestrial Invasive Species
12. Forest Health

---

[1] In the context of this classification system, we use the terms "watershed" and "hydrologic unit" synonymously. Hydrologic units, however, are truly only synonymous with the classic watershed definition when their boundaries include all the source areas contributing surface water to a single, defined outlet point. For the intended uses of this reconnaisance-level assessment, this distinction is relatively unimportant.

The Watershed Condition Model

The basic model used in this classification system provides a forestwide, reconnaissance-level evaluation of watershed condition. It offers a systematic, flexible means of classifying and comparing watersheds based on a core set of national watershed condition indicators. The indicators are grouped according to four major **process categories**: (1) aquatic physical, (2) aquatic biological, (3) terrestrial physical, and (4) terrestrial biological (fig.1). These categories represent terrestrial, riparian, and aquatic ecosystem processes or mechanisms by which management actions can affect the condition of watersheds and associated resources.

We will use a simple score card approach to assess watershed condition class. Each of the four process categories is represented by a set of indicators (fig. 2, table 1). Each indicator is evaluated using a defined set of attributes. For example, the Aquatic Physical Processes category contains an indicator for Aquatic Habitat Condition. Aquatic habitat condition is evaluated using three attributes: (1) habitat fragmentation, (2) large woody debris, and (3) channel shape and function. Indicators can have as few as one attribute or as many as four attributes. We designed the classification to be as simple as possible based on the "80/20 Rule," which states that often 80 percent of

effects come from 20 percent of the causes. We also wanted to be responsive to user input obtained during pilot testing on national forests to keep the assessment compatible with the subjective nature of many of the evaluations. We therefore constrained the number of attributes and consequently the amount of data that national forest ID teams will need to deal with during the classification process.

We recognize from a scientific perspective that this watershed conditions model with its many indicators will have problems with autocorrelation. Because of the management need to show linkages between activities on the ground and improvement in watershed condition for performance accountability, however, we chose to include a comprehensive suite of indicators that represents the full scope of Forest Service management activities and program areas. For example, road condition and stream habitat condition may be highly correlated, however, eliminating stream habitat condition as an indicator would then preclude having a feedback mechanism for taking credit for watershed condition improvements derived from stream habitat improvement work. Using a comprehensive set of indicators favors management performance tracking and accountability at the expense of a more scientifically correct classification model.

Figure 1.—*The basic watershed condition model.*

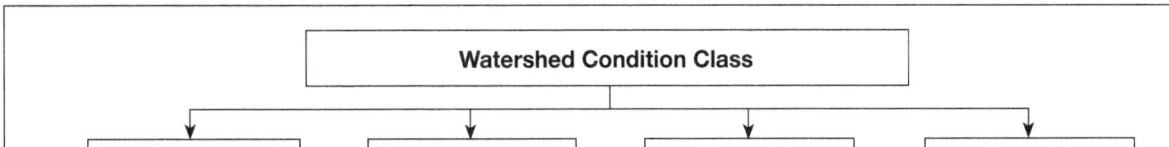

Figure 2.—*Core national watershed condition indicators.*

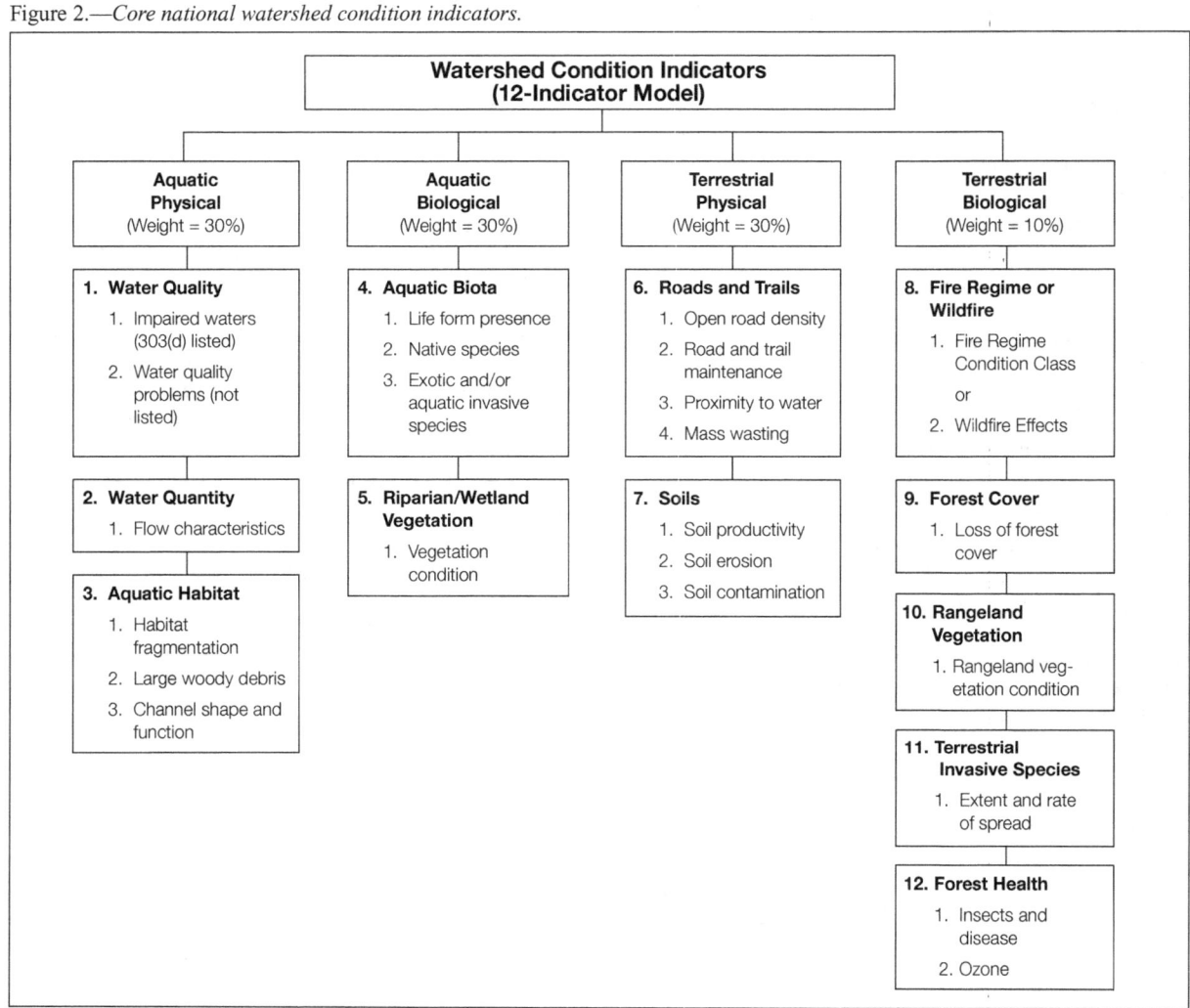

**Watershed Condition Indicators
(12-Indicator Model)**

**Aquatic
Physical**
(Weight = 30%)

**Aquatic
Biological**
(Weight = 30%)

**Terrestrial
Physical**
(Weight = 30%)

**Terrestrial
Biological**
(Weight = 10%)

1. Water Quality
1. Impaired waters (303(d) listed)
2. Water quality problems (not listed)

2. Water Quantity
1. Flow characteristics

3. Aquatic Habitat
1. Habitat fragmentation
2. Large woody debris
3. Channel shape and function

4. Aquatic Biota
1. Life form presence
2. Native species
3. Exotic and/or aquatic invasive species

5. Riparian/Wetland Vegetation
1. Vegetation condition

6. Roads and Trails
1. Open road density
2. Road and trail maintenance
3. Proximity to water
4. Mass wasting

7. Soils
1. Soil productivity
2. Soil erosion
3. Soil contamination

8. Fire Regime or Wildfire
1. Fire Regime Condition Class
or
2. Wildfire Effects

9. Forest Cover
1. Loss of forest cover

10. Rangeland Vegetation
1. Rangeland veg-etation condition

11. Terrestrial Invasive Species
1. Extent and rate of spread

12. Forest Health
1. Insects and disease
2. Ozone

Table 1.—*Description of the 12 national core watershed condition indicators. (See the appendix for the complete rule set.)*

Aquatic Physical Indicators	
1. Water Quality	This indicator addresses the expressed alteration of physical, chemical, and biological components of water quality.
2. Water Quantity	This indicator addresses changes to the natural flow regime with respect to the magnitude, duration, or timing of the natural streamflow hydrograph.
3. Aquatic Habitat	This indicator addresses aquatic habitat condition with respect to habitat fragmentation, large woody debris, and channel shape and function.
Aquatic Biological Indicators	
4. Aquatic Biota	This indicator addresses the distribution, structure, and density of native and introduced aquatic fauna.
5. Riparian/Wetland Vegetation	This indicator addresses the function and condition of riparian vegetation along streams, water bodies, and wetlands.
Terrestrial Physical Indicators	
6. Roads and Trails	This indicator addresses changes to the hydrologic and sediment regimes because of the density, location, distribution, and maintenance of the road and trail network.
7. Soils	This indicator addresses alteration to natural soil condition, including productivity, erosion, and chemical contamination.
Terrestrial Biological Indicators	
8. Fire Regime or Wildfire	This indicator addresses the potential for altered hydrologic and sediment regimes because of departures from historical ranges of variability in vegetation, fuel composition, fire frequency, fire severity, and fire pattern.
9. Forest Cover	This indicator addresses the potential for altered hydrologic and sediment regimes because of the loss of forest cover on forest lands.
10. Rangeland Vegetation	This indicator addresses effects on soil and water because of the vegetative health of rangelands.
11. Terrestrial Invasive Species	This indicator addresses potential effects on soil, vegetation, and water resources because of terrestrial invasive species (including vertebrates, invertebrates, and plants).
12. Forest Health	This indicator addresses forest mortality effects on hydrologic and soil function because of major invasive and native forest insect and disease outbreaks and air pollution.

Types of Indicators

We define indicators as simple quantifiable or qualitatively determined measures of the condition and dynamics of broader, more complex attributes of ecosystem health. We use indicators because complex ecosystem attributes are difficult, inconvenient, or too expensive to measure. Indicators act as surrogates, representing the underlying ecological processes that maintain watershed functionality and condition. The basic watershed condition uses indicators that represent existing, on-the-ground alterations of watershed conditions. We will refine the indicators over time as better data and analysis tools become available.

The indicators include three basic types of attributes:

1. **Numeric attributes** have associated numeric values (e.g., road density <1 mile/mile^2). Quantitative attributes are simple to use but they need to be properly interpreted and appropriate for the geographical setting of the watershed.

2. **Descriptive attributes** are qualitative variables subject to some degree of interpretation by users (e.g., "Native mid to late seral vegetation appropriate to the sites potential dominates the plant communities and is vigorous, healthy, and diverse in age, structure, cover, and composition on more than 80 percent of the riparian and wetland areas in the watershed."). These semiquantitative attributes are typically used when reliable numeric indicators or thresholds are lacking or where quantitative data is either unavailable or too expensive to obtain for entire watersheds.

3. **Map-derived attributes** are produced by teams of experts that synthesize extensive data to create interpreted map products (e.g., Fire Regime Condition Classes). Map products

are generally high quality and objective if applied at the appropriate scale.

We anticipate that map-based and numeric indicators will eventually replace other indicators as better data become available.

Indicator Limitations and the Need for Professional Judgment

Good indicator sets should be comprehensive, accurately reflect watershed functionality, be readily measurable, be repeatable, provide data that we can unambiguously interpret, convey an understanding of how the ecosystem functions, and provide insight into the cause-and-effect relationships between environmental stressors and the response of the ecosystem (Mulder et al. 1999). Indicator sets, however, rarely exhibit all of these characteristics. Our application of indicators in this guide does not provide the level of detail expected from site-specific watershed analysis or assessments (USDA/USDI 1998), nor is it intended as a comprehensive evaluation of ecological conditions. Much like the Dow Jones Index gauges the strength of the stock market, watershed condition indicators rapidly assess the relative health of watersheds at a reconnaissance level. We will need additional detailed assessments to validate conclusions, to identify specific watershed problems, and to arrive at treatment solutions.

As simple surrogates for complex ecological processes, indicators do not necessarily represent cause-and-effect relationships. Indicators are derived from studies that correlate the behavior of indicators with environmental response variables of interest. For example, increasing road density has been correlated with increasing sediment yield in many studies nationwide. However, the true set of environmental conditions that produce sedimentation are complex, unmeasured, or unknown. Numerous other factors including soils, geology, slope, and road condition also influence sediment yield. The result is that road density is not a perfect predictor of the effects on sediment yield. The quality of an indicator ultimately depends on the quality of the research used to support it and its applicability to different environmental settings, but no single indicator is a perfect predictor of an environmental response.

Indicators work best when they are applied within the set of conditions under which they were developed, and the same indicator will have different interpretations in different ecological settings. For example, the naturally low volumes of large woody debris in many streams of the arid Southwest would represent degraded conditions in the forests of western Oregon. Even the map-based indicators such as Fire Regime Condition Class, which have been developed for the entire United States, are subject to local professional validation and interpretation to ensure that they are correctly applied. When used inappropriately, indicators and their attributes can provide misleading or incorrect conclusions. Numeric values should not be thought of as absolutes, but rather as diagnostic tools to promote discussion and understanding of relative watershed condition with respect to the rule set. *As a result, this process relies on local professional expertise and judgment to interpret the indicators and assess watershed condition.*[2]

Providing for National Consistency and Local Flexibility

Professional judgment is needed to properly interpret the indicators, but a certain level of consistency is needed to compare watersheds at the national level. Achieving consistent evaluation is a challenge when applying professional judgment across diverse ecosystems. To improve consistency, the WCC system uses specific attributes along with quantitative and qualitative rule sets to assess watershed condition. This structured approach, coupled with appropriate regional office oversight is designed to minimize bias among evaluators and promote consistent interpretation of indicators.

Interpreting indicators, however, also requires local flexibility, because only a few simple indicators have numeric ranges of values that we can uniformly apply nationwide. For example, the natural range of water temperatures will have different values in warm water streams compared with high elevation trout streams, but an interpreted threshold specific to each environment indicates impairment. In addition, not all indicators apply in all environmental conditions and geophysical settings. For example, mass movement processes in the mountainous West are virtually nonexistent in the Lake States of the Midwest.

To provide the needed flexibility, the WCC system allows limited adjustment of core indicator attributes based on local data and conditions. To help maintain consistency, regional or national oversight teams need to approve these adjustments.

---

[2] This process relies on intuitive conclusions and predictions that are dependent on an analyst's training, interpretation of facts, information, and observations and on his or her personal knowledge of the watershed being analyzed. Professional judgment in this context is excercised by a national forest's interdisciplinary team.

The goal of the process is to use the best available information and data to assess watershed condition and to interpret the range of watershed conditions in different physiographic settings in a correct and conceptually similar manner relative to the range of proper and impaired functionality.

Forests may adjust attributes in one of three ways:

1. **Modify the default values of an attribute.** For example, the default ranges in the basic model for road density may be inappropriate for certain physiographic settings. Forests may adjust the range and breaks between good, fair, and poor ratings if they are supported by forest plans or local analysis and data.

2. **Substitute high-quality attribute data where appropriate.** For example, a forest may have extensive Properly Functioning Condition survey data that could be used to rate attributes associated with the Riparian Vegetation Condition indicator. Alternatively, the Alaska Region, may wish to substitute riparian forest age class structure as their indicator of riparian vegetation condition.

3. **Rate an attribute as Not Applicable.** For example, a forest lacking rangelands and grazing lands may exclude rangeland vegetation from their assessment of the terrestrial physical process category. A *Not Applicable (N/A)* rating can also be used for indicators or attributes not relevant within a particular geographical context. Only two indicators (Forest Cover and Rangeland Vegetation) and two attributes (large woody debris and mass wasting) may be rated N/A subject to Regional Oversight Team approval.

Limited attribute adjustments provide the flexibility needed to account for local differences in individual watersheds while maintaining an acceptable level of regional and national consistency. National consistency in scoring is maintained by retaining a consistent set of indicators, averaging attribute scores within each indicator, and weight-averaging indicator scores by process category. National consistency is most important at the process category level because each forest ID team evaluates these fundamental ecosystem process categories in a manner appropriate to their geographic setting.

We anticipate that there will be instances, or locally unique circumstances, where the computed condition rating may not accurately reflect true on-the-ground conditions. In these cases, forests can exercise an "override option" and replace the computed condition rating with the condition class judged to be correct. Typically, the override option would be used to

designate severely impaired watersheds. Examples where the override option might be appropriate include situations such as (1) acid streams totally devoid of biological life, (2) water quality impairment because of chemical contamination, or (3) streams that are totally dewatered by diversions. In all of these examples, the upland areas may be in excellent condition but the water body is clearly impaired.

ID teams should use the override option judiciously and rarely. Exercising the override option will require written documentation and approval from the Regional Oversight Team. The National Oversight Team will review use of the override option annually to ensure that it is being applied in an appropriate manner.

Classifying Individual Indicators

Each indicator attribute receives a rating. The ratings are expressions of the "best-fit" descriptor of the attribute for the entire 6th-level watershed being classified. In the absence of established numeric criteria for most of the attributes, the boundaries between the attribute condition ratings were assigned by resource specialists working on the Watershed Condition Advisory Team using professional judgment guided by the conceptual condition descriptions below.

Condition Rating 1 is synonymous with "GOOD" condition. It is the expected indicator value in a watershed with high geomorphic, hydrologic, and biotic integrity relative to natural potential condition. The rating suggests that the watershed is functioning properly with respect to that attribute.

Condition Rating 2 is synonymous with "FAIR" condition. It is the expected indicator value in a watershed with moderate geomorphic, hydrologic, and biotic integrity relative to natural potential condition. The rating suggests that the watershed is functioning at risk with respect to that attribute.

Condition Rating 3 is synonymous with "POOR" condition. It is the expected indicator value in a watershed with low geomorphic, hydrologic, and biotic integrity relative to natural potential condition. The rating suggests that the watershed is impaired or functioning at unacceptable risk with respect to that attribute.

To conceptualize this, the suggested approach is to identify the upper and lower bounds for each indicator attribute to differentiate the desired conditions for that attribute (high integrity or high functionality relative to site potential) compared with the unacceptable or impaired functionality of the attribute in absolute terms. Conceptually, identifying the end points should be the easiest task to accomplish in any rating scheme. The remaining middle designation is then identified by default and may contain a wide range of conditions. Ratings are scaled and evaluated in an absolute sense from functioning properly to impaired function and not relative to a more limited range of attribute conditions that may occur on a particular national forest.

The complete watershed condition rule set for indicators and attributes is contained in the appendix. For each indicator, we provide a brief statement of purpose, the rule set to use to determine the condition rating of each attribute, additional guidance pertaining to rating the indicator attributes, definitions, a brief rationale of how the indicator relates to watershed condition, and references. Careful reading of the "Additional Guidance" section for each indicator is essential for appropriate use of the rule set.

The example below illustrates the process of scoring an individual indicator on Forest Service lands. The example indicator is Roads and Trails Condition. The hypothetical watershed is in the upper Midwest, which has no unstable landforms susceptible to mass wasting. The watershed is heavily roaded, with a road density of 2.5 mi/mi². Roads are well maintained but more than 25 percent are within 100 feet of water. The forest ID team decides that mass wasting is not an issue in this watershed and assigned the following ratings to road condition:

Roads and trails attributes	Rating	Explanation
Open road density	3	Poor (impaired function)
Road maintenance	2	Fair (functioning at risk)
Proximity to water	3	Poor (impaired function)
Mass wasting	N/A	N/A (the watershed is not susceptible to mass wasting)
Indicator rating	**2.7**	Poor (impaired function)

The complete classification process for each watershed is described below:

1. For each 6th-level HUC watershed, all attributes for each of the 12 indicators are scored by the forest ID team as 1 (Good—Functioning Properly), 2 (Fair—Functioning at Risk), or 3 (Poor—Impaired Function) using written criteria and rule sets and the best available data and professional judgment.

2. The attribute scores for each indicator are summed and averaged to produce an indicator score.

3. The indicator scores within each ecosystem process category are then averaged to arrive at a process category score.

4. The overall watershed condition score is computed as a weighted[3] average of the four process category scores.

5. The watershed condition scores are tracked to one decimal point and reported as Watershed Condition Classes 1, 2, or 3. Class 1 = scores of 1.0 to 1.6, Class 2 = scores from 1.7 to 2.2, and Class 3 = scores from 2.3 to 3.0.

6. A separate scoring process is conducted for Forest Service and non-Forest Service lands within the watershed. We will report results for Forest Service and non-Forest Service lands and a watershed composite overall watershed condition score (area weighted average of Forest Service and non-Forest Service lands).

We will assign condition ratings to Forest Service ownerships, private lands, and the composite watershed. The composite score rates the whole watershed and includes FS and all other ownerships, which are typically private land. The intent is to differentiate watershed conditions attributable to Forest Service management and problems that the FS can solve from those that are associated with others. We also wish to support the Secretary's call for an "all lands" approach to resource management.

Because we frequently lack data about the condition of non-Forest Service lands, a simpler approach is applied to these ownerships. We will assign non-Forest Service lands a subjective rating on a whole-watershed basis (i.e., we will not score individual indicators and attributes). Non-Forest Service lands will be rated as either THE SAME AS, BETTER THAN, or POORER THAN Forest Service lands in the watershed. If SAME AS is selected, we will assign the non-Forest Service lands the same numeric condition score as Forest Service lands. If non-Forest Service lands are not the same as Forest Service lands, we will designate the non-Forest Service lands as simply Class 1, Class 2, or Class 3 based on the best available knowledge. Forests are encouraged to rate non-Forest Service lands equal to Forest Service lands if the true condition is unknown. Forests may work with partner groups to classify non-Forest Service lands, if they wish.

National forests will complete the classification process using the Watershed Classification and Assessment Tracking Tool (WCATT), a Web-based application developed by the natural resource manager program staff.

---

[3] We weight process categories to reflect their relative contribution toward watershed condition from a national perspective. The aquatic physical and aquatic biological categories are weighted at 30 percent each because of their direct impact to aquatic systems (endpoint indicators). The terrestrial physical category is weighted at 30 percent because roads are typically one of the highest sources of impact to watershed condition. Terrestrial biological is weighted at 10 percent because these indicators have indirect impact to watershed condition.

Regional and National Oversight

This classification process relies on Washington Office and regional office oversight to provide for flexibility and consistency in application among national forests. The Washington Office technical oversight role will be the primary responsibility of the Watershed, Fish, Wildlife, Air, and Rare Plants program staff, who will be assisted by members of the Watershed Condition Advisory Team because of the interdisciplinary nature of the classification process. Advisory team members will provide technical input, expertise, and advice regarding the rule sets affecting their program areas.

The Washington Office will coordinate an annual meeting to discuss technical classification issues and resolve disputes. This will include, as a minimum, a review of the extent to which regions permitted use of "Not Applicable" and the "Override" options.

National oversight roles and responsibilities include—

1. Managing the national change process for the classification system.

2. Ensuring consistency of classification among the regions.

3. Providing and supporting development of national GIS data products for use in classification.

4. Providing direction and resolving disputes between regions.

Regions will provide the first line of quality control and quality assurance in the classification process. Regions are encouraged to work collectively with their forests to discuss interpretations of the rule-set wording to achieve as much consistency as practicable among forest units. Regions may wish to develop regional additional guidance supplements to this guide that document local application, data sources, and interpretations. The membership of Regional Office Oversight Teams is left to the discretion of the regions.

Regional oversight roles and responsibilities include—

1. Ensuring consistency of classification among the forests in the region.

2. Ensuring that forests use ID teams to perform classifications.

3. Approving use or modification to attribute default value, substituting high-quality attribute data or alternative wording for attributes, and the use of the "Not Applicable" and "Override" options.

4. Coordinating classification with adjoining regions and national forests.

5. Consulting with the Washington Office when significant modifications are approved.

Procedural Guidance

We specifically designed this watershed classification approach as a rapid, coarse filter, office assessment process to be completed by a forest ID team over a 2-week time period using professional judgment relying on existing information, maps, and GIS coverage.

Preparation Checklist

1. Identify the composition and leadership of the forest ID team that will classify watershed condition. Consider having someone from the forest land and resource planning staff as the team leader. The team should include technical specialists with expertise in the 12 condition indicator program areas. Typically, a forest ID team will do the classification, but forests may include district staffs. Specialists with long tenure and familiarity with the forest can prove especially valuable to the team because of the breadth of experience they provide.

2. Designate a technical lead for each of the watershed condition indicators. For example, a hydrologist might lead water-quality and water-quantity assessments.

3. Have each specialist review the rule set and additional guidance for his or her indicator to help him or her understand the types of data and information that are useful to rate the attributes for that indicator.

4. Over a 1-week period, have each specialist assemble the available information in preparation for the classification process. The types of information will vary by discipline and may include forest inventory and monitoring reports, interpreted map products, or assessments done by others.

5. Arrange for support from forest GIS specialists who can provide analysis support (e.g., road density, and road proximity to water analysis) that summarizes data by 6th-level HUCs. Obtain the most current national GIS data

coverage that is relevant to the analysis such as 303(d) impaired streams, Fire Regime Condition Class, and insect and disease maps, as well as local GIS data such as roads and trails, dams and diversions, active and abandoned mines, forest cover, recent large fires, etc.

6. Have each technical specialist develop a preliminary rating for his or her indicator for each 6th-level HUC that can be brought forward to the ID team for discussion.

Classification Process Checklist

1. Allow at least 1 week (5 days) for the ID team to complete the classification process.

2. Convene the ID team and discuss the rule set for classification with the intent of achieving a common understanding. At this time, the team should also discuss and reach agreement on any indicators and/or attributes (forest cover, rangelands, mass wasting, large woody debris) that they may wish to designate as "Not Applicable" to the particular forest, any proposed changes to attribute thresholds (e.g., road density), or substitution of alternative attribute wording for some indicators. Before the actual meeting, discuss and obtain approval from your Regional Oversight Team, if necessary.

3. Determine ratings using an interactive ID team process. Individual specialists may offer their preliminary classification of an indicator rating score, but the team should pool its collective knowledge to arrive at the final rating. The process will go slowly for the first few watersheds as individuals begin to gain a common understanding of the rating approach, and it may take several hours to classify the first watershed. Consider beginning with a watershed known to be in good condition and then rate one known to be in poor condition to help provide perspective on the range of existing conditions. The process will speed up noticeably after several iterations.

4. Use Tom Brown's national watershed risk-rating maps (Brown and Froemke 2010) as the forest's beginning point for classifying watershed condition. The national rating will provide perspective regarding the spatial distribution of watershed condition and illustrate how the local forest ratings fit within the context of national ratings. Remember that Brown and Froemke's work assesses risk and is based on broad-scale 5th-level HUCs using nationally consistent coarse-scale data that are not particularly applicable to forest management activities so they may not match well with your local conditions.

5. Use the Watershed Condition Classification Tool (WCATT) to record ratings and capture notes. Display the WCATT form on a large screen. A second large screen display may be useful to display other relevant GIS data layers.

Annual and Periodic Reassessments

1. Forests will need to update watershed condition classifications each year to track changes in watershed condition class for performance accountability. Concentrate on reassessing those watersheds that are known or suspected to have changed significantly from the previous year, focusing on—

   a. Priority watersheds where improvement activities have been implemented.

   b. Watersheds that have experienced large fires since the previous year.

   c. Watersheds that have experienced extensive natural disturbance. To facilitate annual updates, the WCATT has been designed to roll forward the previous year's classification data into the current year and forests will need to modify only those watersheds that have changed.

2. Conduct a more rigorous classification of all watersheds every 5 years, or sooner if conditions warrant. In all cases, use an ID team to perform annual and periodic reassessments.

References

Bailey, R.G. 1995. Description of the ecoregions of the United States. 2nd ed., rev. Misc. Pub. No. 1391.Washington, DC: U.S. Department of Agriculture, Forest Service. 77 p. http://www.fs.fed.us/land/ecosysmgmt/ecoreg1_home.html. (24 March 2011).

Brown, T.C.; Froemke, P. 2010. Risk of impaired condition of watersheds containing national forest lands. Gen. Tech. Rep. RMRS-GTR-251. Fort Collins, CO: U.S. Department of Agriculture, Forest Service, Rocky Mountain Research Station. 57 p.

Heller, D. 2004. A paradigm shift in watershed restoration. Forum for Research and Extension in Natural Resources (FORREX), Streamline Watershed Management Bulletin. 8(1): 21–23. http://www.forrex.org/streamline/ISS28/streamline_vol8_no1_art7.pdf. (25 March 2011).

Karr, J.R.; Chu, L.W. 1999. Restoring life in running rivers: better biological monitoring. Washington, DC: Island Press. 206 p.

Lackey, R.T. 2001. Values, policy, and ecosystem health. Bioscience. 51: 437–443.

Mulder, B.; Noon, B.R.; Spies, T.A., et al. 1999. The strategy and design of the effectiveness monitoring program for the Northwest Forest Plan. Gen. Tech. Rep. PNW-GTR-437. Washington, DC: U.S. Department of Agriculture, Forest Service.

National Research Council. 1999. New strategies for America's watersheds. Committee on Watershed Management. Washington, DC: National Academy Press. 328 p.

Newbold, S.C. 2002. Integrated modeling for watershed management: multiple objectives and spatial effects. Journal of the American Water Resources Association. 38(2): 341–353.

Ogg, C.W.; Keith, G.A. 2002. New Federal support for priority watershed management needs. Journal of the American Water Resources Association. 38(2): 577–586.

Regier, H.A. 1993. The notion of natural and cultural integrity. In: Woodley, S.J.; Kay, J.J.; Francis, G., eds. Ecological integrity and the management of ecosystems. Delray Beach, FL: St. Lucie Press: 3–18.

Reid, L.M.; Ziemer, R.R.; Furniss, M.J. 1996. Watershed analysis on Federal lands of the Pacific Northwest. Humboldt Interagency Watershed Analysis Center Workshop. McKinleyville, CA. http://www.fs.fed.us/psw/rsl/projects/water/1WhatisWA.htm. (23 August 2010).

Smith, R.D.; Klimas, C.V.; Kleiss, B.A. 2005. A watershed assessment tool for evaluating ecological condition, proposed impacts, and restoration potential at multiple scales. SWWRP Tech. Notes Collection. ERDC TNSWWRP-05-3. Vicksburg, MS: U.S. Army Engineer Research and Development Center.

Suter, G.W. 1993. Critique of ecosystem health concepts and indexes. Environmental Toxicology and Chemistry. 12: 1533–1539.

U.S. Department of Agriculture (USDA). 2010. Strategic plan FY 2010–2015. Washington, DC: U.S. Department of Agriculture. 50 p. http://www.ocfo.usda.gov/usdasp/sp2010/sp2010.pdf. (4 August 2010).

U.S. Department of Agriculture (USDA). 2004. Watershed protection and management. FSM 2520. Washington, DC: U.S. Department of Agriculture, Forest Service. 44 p.

U.S. Department of Agriculture (USDA), Forest Service. 2007 (June 15). An evaluation of watershed condition approaches potentially suitable for characterizing national watershed condition. Watershed Condition Core Team. Washington, DC: Watershed, Fish, Wildlife, Air, and Rare Plants Program. 22 p.

U.S. Department of Agriculture/U.S. Department of the Interior (DOI). 1998. A framework for analyzing the hydrologic condition of watersheds. BLM Tech. Note 405. Washington, DC: U.S. Department of Agriculture, Forest Service; U.S. Department of the Interior, Bureau of Land Management. 37 p.

U.S. Office of Management and Budget (OMB). 2006. Forest Service watershed program assessment. Washington, DC: U.S. Office of Management and Budget. http://www.whitehouse.gov/omb/expectmore/summary/10003029.2006.html. (4 August 2010).

Williams, J.E.; Wood, C.A.; Dombeck, M.P., eds. 1997. Watershed restoration: principles and practices. Bethesda, MD: American Fisheries Society.

Yount, J.D.; Niemi, G.J. 1990. Recovery of lotic communities and ecosystems from disturbance—a narrative case study. Environmental Management. 14: 547–570.

Appendix. Rule Set for Watershed Condition Indicators and Attributes

1. Water Quality Condition

Purpose

This indicator addresses the expressed alteration of physical, biological, or chemical impacts to water quality.

Condition Rating Rule Set

1. Water Quality Condition Indicator	Minimal to no impairment to beneficial uses of the water bodies in the watershed.	Minor impairment to beneficial uses of the water bodies in the watershed.	Significant impairment to beneficial uses of the water bodies in the watershed.
Attributes	**Good (1) Functioning Properly**	**Fair (2) Functioning at Risk**	**Poor (3) Impaired Function**
Impaired waters (303(d) listed)	No State-listed impaired or threatened water bodies.	Less than 10 percent of the stream miles or lake area are listed on the 303(d) or 305(b) lists and are not supporting beneficial uses.	More than 10 percent of the stream miles or lake areas are water quality limited and are not fully supporting beneficial uses as identified by a State water quality agency integrated report (303(d) & 305(b)).
Water quality problems (not listed)	The watershed has minor or no water quality problems. For example, no documented evidence of excessive sediment, nutrients, chemical pollution or other water quality issues above natural or background levels; no consumption advisories or contamination from abandoned or active mines; little or no evidence of acidification, toxicity, or eutrophication because of atmospheric deposition (see "Additional Guidance" related to mines and atmospheric deposition).	The watershed has moderate water quality problems. For example, consumption advisories in localized areas; minor contamination from active or abandoned mines; localized incidence of accelerated sediment, nutrients, chemicals, or infrequent, documented incidents of contamination of public drinking water sources. Moderate evidence of acidification, eutrophication, or toxicity because of atmospheric deposition (see "Additional Guidance" elated to mines and atmospheric deposition).	The watershed has extensive water quality problems. For example, consumption advisories over extended areas; excessive sediment, nutrients, chemicals; extensive contamination from active or abandoned mines; or frequent incidents of contamination of public drinking water sources. Strong evidence of acidification, eutrophication, or toxicity because of atmospheric deposition (see "Additional Guidance" related to mines and atmospheric deposition).

Additional Guidance

1. Water quality should address both surface and ground water.

2. Consider the mainstream systems as indicative of the whole drainage system water quality, (i.e., the composite representative of the condition of all the streams in the watershed).

3. Consider chronic water quality deterioration and short-term effects in light of overall sustained effects to beneficial uses (i.e., both could be irreversible or irretrievable, but are not always so).

4. Consider monitoring and inventory information available from internal and external sources.

5. Because State water quality agency integrated reports (303(d) and 305(b)) are submitted only every 2 years, use the latest and best available information about the status of impaired waters.

6. Atmospheric deposition can affect watersheds by causing acidification (sulfur and nitrogen), eutrophication (nitrogen), or toxicity (mercury). We can use water chemistry or critical loads to classify conditions. A number of sources of water

chemistry data are available (EPA 2006, 2009) and have been compiled into a national database (USDA Forest Service 2009). The most current guidance on using chemistry and critical loads for classification is available at http://www.fs.fed.us/air.

a. For areas where acidification is the major concern, use the following guidance for classification:

i. Condition Rating 1. All water sample sites from the most sensitive water body in the watershed (or a nearby watershed with similar lithology) show an acid neutralizing capacity (ANC) of 50 microequivalents per liter (ueq/L) or greater.

ii. Condition Rating 2. One or more water sample sites from the most sensitive water body in the watershed (or a nearby watershed with similar lithology) show an ANC of greater than 20 ueq/L and less than 50 ueq/L.

iii. Condition Rating 3. One or more water sample sites from the most sensitive water body in the watershed (or a nearby watershed with similar lithology) show an ANC of 20 ueq/L or less.

iv. Water bodies that are naturally acidic (DOC > 5 mg/L) or low in buffering capacity because of the influence of wetlands or local geology should be assigned Condition Rating 1.

v. Where ANC data is lacking, consider rating the attribute using national deposition maps and lithology to find similar watersheds where ANC data is available.

b. In areas where eutrophication (nitrogen) is the primary problem, appropriate classification thresholds set by the U.S. Environmental Protection Agency (EPA) (2010) for each region can be found at www.fs.fed.us/air.

c. Where aquatic critical loads for sulfur or nitrogen are available (such as Sullivan et al. 2007), compare current deposition with the critical load and classify as follows:

i. Condition Rating 1. Sulfur and/or nitrogen deposition is more than 10 percent below the aquatic critical load.

ii. Condition Rating 2. Deposition is 0–10 percent below the aquatic critical load.

iii. Condition Rating 3. Deposition is above the aquatic critical load.

d. For rating water quality effects from abandoned and active mines, use the following guidance for classification:

i. Condition Rating 1. Abandoned and active mines with no associated evidence of water quality contamination.

ii. Condition Rating 2. Abandoned or active mines that have documented evidence of some adverse effects to surface or groundwater quality.

iii. Condition Rating 3. Abandoned or active mines that have been determined to be adversely affecting surface or groundwater as a result of water quality sampling.

Definitions

abandoned mines. Facilities, equipment, material, and associated surface disturbance resulting from past mineral exploration or development, for which there exists no current authorization and no evidence of current owner/operator.

acid neutralizing capacity. A measure of a water body's ability to buffer acid compounds, defined as the difference between cations of strong bases and anions of strong acids.

aquatic organism consumption advisories. Advisories issued by the EPA or by State natural resource or other agencies that advise the public to limit or avoid consumption of certain fish, shellfish, mussels, crayfish, or other aquatic organisms because of pollution. These advisories inform the public that high concentrations of chemical contaminants have been found in local fish and aquatic species and include recommendations to limit or avoid consuming certain fish and wildlife species from specific water bodies.

critical load. The amount of deposition of an atmospheric pollutant below which no harmful ecological effects occur. We can calculate critical loads for both acidity and nutrient nitrogen in terrestrial and aquatic systems.

designated beneficial uses. The desirable uses that water quality should support. Beneficial uses include drinking water supply, primary contact recreation (such as swimming), and aquatic life support. Each designated use has a unique set of water quality requirements or criteria that must be met for the use to be supported. A water body may have multiple beneficial uses. Designated beneficial uses are identified by each State water quality management agency.

eutrophication. Increased growth of biota and a rate of productivity that is accelerated over the rate that would have occurred naturally.

impaired or threatened water body. Any water body that is listed according to section 303(d) of the Clean Water Act. The 303(d) list is a comprehensive public record of all impaired or threatened water bodies, regardless of the cause or source of the impairment or threat. A water body is considered impaired when it does not attain the water quality standards needed to support its designated uses. Standards may be violated because of an individual pollutant, multiple pollutants, thermal pollution, or an unknown cause of impairment. A water body is considered threatened if it currently attains water quality standards, but is predicted to violate standards by the time the next 303(d) list is submitted to EPA. This determination is made by individual State water quality management agencies.

lithology. The gross physical character of a rock or rock formation described in terms of its structure, color, mineral composition, grain size, and arrangement of its component parts; all those visible features that in the aggregate impart individuality to a rock formation.

Rationale for Indicator

Nonpoint source pollution, defined as water pollution that comes from many different sources in a watershed, is the leading remaining cause of water quality problems in the United States. Polluted runoff from agriculture, silvicultural activities, and atmospheric deposition are among the leading causes of nonpoint source pollution problems (EPA 2007). Because nonpoint source pollutants are primarily derived from runoff generated from watershed surfaces, watershed condition and water quality are closely linked. The effects of nonpoint source pollutants on specific waters vary and may not always be fully assessed. We do know, however, that these pollutants have harmful effects on drinking water supplies, recreation, fisheries, and wildlife. In a recent report by EPA (2005), 45 percent of the water bodies assessed by State water quality agencies were reported as impaired or not clean enough to support their designated uses, such as fishing and swimming.

Indicator References

Sullivan, T.J.; Cosby, B.J.; Snyder, K.U., et al 2007. Model-based assessment of the effects of acidic deposition on sensitive watershed resources in the national forests of North Carolina, Tennessee, and South Carolina. http://www.esenvironmental.com/PDF/north_carolina_modeling.pdf. (24 March 2011).

U.S. Department of Agriculture (USDA), Forest Service. 2009. NRIS Air Module. http://www.fs.fed.us/air/. (Forest Service Intranet; accessible only by agency employees.)

U.S. Environmental Protection Agency (EPA). 2006. National stream assessment, wadeable streams assessment: a collaborative survey of the Nation's streams. EPA 841-B-06-002. Washington, DC: EPA. http://water.epa.gov/type/rsl/monitoring/streamsurvey/index.cfm. (24 March 2011).

U.S. Environmental Protection Agency (EPA). 2007 (October). National water quality inventory: report to Congress. 2002 Reporting Cycle. Doc. No. EPA-841-R-07-001. Washington, DC: EPA. http://www.epa.gov/owow/305b/2002report/report2002305b.pdf. (24 March 2011).

U.S. Environmental Protection Agency (EPA). 2010. National lakes assessment: a collaborative survey of the Nation's lakes. EPA 841-R-09-001. Washington, DC: EPA, Office of Water and Office of Research and Development. http://water.epa.gov/type/lakes/lakessurvey_index.cfm. (24 March 2011).

2. Water Quantity Condition

Purpose

This indicator addresses changes to the natural flow regime with respect to the magnitude, duration, or timing of natural streamflow hydrographs.

Condition Rating Rule Set

2. Water Quantity Condition Indicator	Stream hydrographs have no or minor departure from natural conditions.	Stream hydrographs have moderate recognized departures from natural conditions part of the year.	The magnitude, duration, and/or timing of annual extreme flows (low and/or high) significantly depart from the natural hydrograph.
Attributes	**Good (1) Functioning Properly**	**Fair (2) Functioning at Risk**	**Poor (3) Impaired Function**
Flow characteristics	The watershed lacks significant man-made reservoirs, dams, or diversion facilities. The watershed has primarily free-flowing rivers and streams, unmodified lakes, and no or limited ground water withdrawals. Stream hydrographs have no or minor alterations from natural (unaltered by anthropogenic actions) conditions.	The watershed contains dams and diversion facilities that are operated to partially mimic natural hydrographs. A departure from a natural hydrograph occurs during periods other than extreme flows (lows or highs). Peaks and base flows are maintained but changes to the timing, rate of change, and/or duration of mid-range discharges occur.	Dams and diversion facilities are operated so that they fail to mimic natural hydrographs. The magnitude, duration, and/or timing of annual extreme flows (low or high) significantly depart from the natural hydrograph. The timing and the rate of change in flows often do not correlate with expected seasonal changes.

Additional Guidance

1. Compare existing conditions with historic conditions and reference conditions. The natural hydrograph baseline is streamflows unaltered by anthropogenic actions. Emphasis is on the permanent, long-term effects of water diversions and water control features rather than on flow changes caused by vegetation management.

2. Consider both the mainstream and tributaries when evaluating changes to flow hydrology. In most cases, depending on their extent and magnitude, cumulative changes observable in the mainstream stream will reflect flow changes to tributaries.

3. Concentrate evaluation on effects to perennial, mainstream streams rather than headwater tributaries or intermittent flows, except in arid or semiarid regions where intermittent or interrupted flows are important components of the hydrograph.

4. The effect on water quantity condition should be significant enough so that it results in measurable changes to the hydrograph. For example, water yield changes resulting from vegetation management would generally not be included unless the change was extensive and prolonged (e.g., extensive deforestation, urbanization, wildfire, dams, diversions, disease, insects, or other disturbances that significantly and persistently alter runoff).

5. The extent of groundwater pumping would generally need to be developed for large-scale industrial or large municipality use to measurably influence streamflow. In general, household groundwater use for domestic purposes will not have a significant influence on water quantity unless a watershed was developed to such an extent that it was closed to additional well developments by State water resource authorities.

6. Consider the effects of transbasin diversions with respect to both the donor and receiving streams.

Definitions

natural hydrograph. A hydrograph representing the natural seasonal flows of a river without the moderating influence of human-created features (e.g., dams and canals) or management actions.

Rationale for Indicator

Watershed condition has large role to play in the magnitude, frequency, and timing of runoff from a watershed. The quantity and timing of streamflow are critical components of water supply, water quality, and the ecological integrity of river systems (Hill et al. 1991). The effects of human alteration on the natural flow regimes of rivers and ecological processes are now reasonably well understood (Poff et al. 1997). Modifying natural hydrologic processes disrupts the dynamic equilibrium between the movement of water and the movement of sediment that exists in free-flowing rivers (Dunne and Leopold 1978). This disruption alters physical habitat characteristics, including water temperature, oxygen content, water chemistry, and substrate composition, and adversely changes the composition, structure, or function of aquatic, riparian, and wetland ecosystems (Bain et al. 1988). The result is that many rivers no longer support socially valued native species or sustain healthy ecosystems (NRC 1992).

Indicator References

Bain, M.B.; Finn, J.T.; Booke, H.E. 1988. Stream flow regulation and fish community structure. Ecology. 69: 382–392.

Dunne, T.; Leopold, L.B. 1978. Water in environmental planning. San Francisco: W.H. Freeman. 818 p.

Hill, M.T.; Platts, W.S.; Beschta, R.L. 1991. Ecological and geomorphological concepts for instream and out-of-channel flow requirements. Rivers. 2: 198–210.

National Research Council (NRC). 1992. Restoration of aquatic systems: science, technology, and public policy. Washington, DC: National Academy Press. 576 p.

Poff, N.L.; Allan, J.D.; Bain, M.B., et al. 1997. The natural flow regime: a paradigm for river conservation and restoration. BioScience. 47(11): 769–784.

3. Aquatic Habitat Condition

Purpose

This indicator addresses aquatic habitat condition with respect to habitat fragmentation, large woody debris, and channel shape and function.

Condition Rating Rule Set

3. Aquatic Habitat Condition Indicator	The watershed supports large continuous blocks of high-quality aquatic habitat and high-quality stream channel conditions.	The watershed supports medium to small blocks of contiguous habitat. Some high-quality aquatic habitat is available, but stream channel conditions show signs of being degraded.	The watershed supports small amounts of continuous high-quality aquatic habitat. Most stream channel conditions show evidence of being degraded by disturbance.
Attributes	**Good (1) Functioning Properly**	**Fair (2) Functioning at Risk**	**Poor (3) Impaired Function**
Habitat fragmentation (including aquatic organism passage)	Habitat fragmentation is not a serious concern (more than 95 percent of historic aquatic habitats are still connected).	Aquatic habitat fragmentation is increasing because of temperature, aquatic organism passage blockages, or dewatering (only 25 to 95 percent of the historic aquatic habitats are still connected).	Aquatic habitat fragmentation because of temperature, blockages, or dewatering is a serious concern (less than 25 percent of the historic aquatic habitats still connected).
Large woody debris	In aquatic and riparian systems that evolved with wood near the streams, large woody debris is present and continues to be recruited into the system at near natural rates.	In aquatic and riparian systems that evolved with wood, large woody debris is present but is recruited into the system at less than natural rates because of riparian management activities.	In a system that should contain large wood as an ecosystem component, wood is lacking resulting in poor riparian or aquatic habitat conditions including bank destabilization, inadequate pool formation, and microclimate maintenance.
Channel shape and function	Channel width-to-depth ratios exhibit the range of conditions expected in the absence of human influence. Less than 5 percent of the stream channels show signs of widening. Channels are vertically stable, with isolated locations of aggradation or degradation, which would be expected in near-natural conditions. The distribution of channels with floodplain connectivity is close to that found in reference watersheds of similar size and geology.	Channel width-to-depth and vertical stability are maintained except where riparian vegetation has been disturbed. Between 5 and 25 percent of the stream channel have seen an increase in width-to-depth ratios. Channel degradation and/or aggradation are evident but limited to relatively small sections of the channel network. There is evidence of downcutting to the extent that some stream channels are no longer connected to their floodplain.	More than 25 percent of channels have width-to-depth ratios greater than expected under near-natural conditions. The size and extent of gullied sections of channels are extensive, currently increasing, or have increased recently. Many streambanks show signs of active erosion above that which is expected naturally. Channel degradation and/or aggradation are evident and widespread because of unstable streambeds and banks. Many (more than 50 percent) of the stream channels are disconnected from their floodplain or are braided channels because of increased sediment loads.

Additional Guidance

1. If forest plan aquatic habitat direction exists for habitat fragmentation, large wood, or channel shape and function, use the local thresholds derived from forest plan standards and guidelines to determine the appropriate rating for the attributes.

2. The focus of this evaluations should be on fish bearing channels lower in the watershed that are typically response reaches (<3 percent gradient). Consider the length of these reaches in the watershed, and estimate the length of channel that meets the criteria for the class.

3. Large woody debris. Rate this attribute Not Applicable (N/A) if the aquatic and riparian systems in the watershed

evolved without wood and if the presence of wood is not an important component of the aquatic ecosystem. The use of N/A will likely be limited to western rangeland watersheds.

4. In aquatic habitats lacking aquatic biota and/or permanent habitat (e.g., some Southwest desert streams), evaluate conditions with respect to what you would expected to be present under natural conditions, or absent human-induced impacts.

Definitions

aquatic habitat fragmentation. Habitat fragmentation occurs when a large region of habitat has been degraded or fragmented into a collection of smaller patches of nonconnected habitat. Major causes of aquatic habitat fragmentation are dams, diversions, mines, roads, inadequate culverts, and increased stream temperatures that prevent fish from moving freely throughout an aquatic system.

floodplain connectivity. In channels with existing or historic floodplains, floodplain connectivity refers to the ability of flows greater than bankfull to overflow on to the vegetated floodplain without accelerated impact to streambanks. Floodplain connectivity may be lost through the construction of levees, or through the downcutting of channels because of improper road location and construction, overgrazing, storage dams, or increased flow or sediment. Incised channels lack floodplain connectivity.

response channel reaches. Low gradient (in general, less than 3 percent) transport-limited channels in which significant morphologic adjustment occurs in response to increased sediment supply as defined by Montgomery and Buffington (1993). Response channels generally correspond to Rosgen C, D, E, and F channel types (Rosgen 1996). Response reaches are evaluated because they are the most susceptible to change from disturbance.

Rationale for Indicator

Watersheds in good condition tend to retain most of their natural heterogeneity and complexity such as preserving the lateral, longitudinal, and vertical connections between system components as well as the natural spatial and temporal variability of these components (Naiman et al. 1992). Floodplain connectivity demonstrates maintenance of the vertical component of stream channels and provides for off-channel habitat among other features. Habitat fragmentation evaluates the longitudinal component of healthy systems. Aquatic habitat fragmentation by fish passage blockages, dewatering, or temperature increases, along with simplification from activities including channelization, channel bed sedimentation, woody debris removal, and flow regulation, results in loss of diversity within and among native fish species (Lee et al. 1997). Maintaining heterogeneous and complex aquatic organism habitat at multiple scales is recognized as an important influence on species diversity and ecosystem stability (Sedell et al. 1990).

Indicator References

Lee, D.C., et al. 1997. An assessment of ecosystem components in the Interior Columbia Basin and portions of the Klamath and Great Basin. Broadscale assessment of aquatic species and habitats. Gen. Tech. Rep. PNW-GTR-405. Portland, OR: U.S. Department of Agriculture, Forest Service. Vol. 3.

Montgomery, D.R.; Buffington, J.M. 1993. Channel classification, prediction of channel response, and assessment of channel condition. Rep. TFW-SH10-93-002. Prepared for the SHAMW Committee of Washington State Timber/Fish/Wildlife Agreement. Seattle, WA: University of Washington. 84 p.

Naiman, R.J.; Beechie, T.J.; Benda, L.E., et al. 1992. Fundamental elements of ecologically healthy watersheds in the Pacific Northwest coastal ecoregion. In: Naiman, R.D., ed. Watershed management: balancing sustainability and environmental change. New York: Springer-Verlag: 127–188.

Rosgen, D.L. 1996. Applied river morphology. Pagosa Springs, CO: Wildland Hydrology. 390 p.

Sedell, J.R.; Reeves, G.H.; Hauer, F.R., et al. 1990. Role of refugia in recovery from disturbances: modern fragmented and disconnected river systems. Environmental Management. 14(5): 711–724.

4. Aquatic Biota Condition

Purpose

This indicator addresses the distribution, structure, and density of native and introduced aquatic fauna.

Condition Rating Rule Set

4. Aquatic Biota Condition Indicator	All native aquatic communities and life histories appropriate to the site and watershed are present and self-maintaining.	The watershed is a stronghold for one or more native aquatic communities when compared to other sub-basins within the native range. Some life histories may have been lost or range has been reduced within the watershed.	The watershed may support small, wildly scattered populations of native aquatic species. Exotic and/or aquatic invasive species are pervasive.
Attributes	**Good (1) Functioning Properly**	**Fair (2) Functioning at Risk**	**Poor (3) Impaired Function**
Life form presence	More than 90 percent of expected aquatic life forms and communities are present based on the potential natural communities present.	From 70 to 90 percent of expected aquatic life forms and communities are present based on the potential natural communities present.	Less than 70 percent of expected aquatic life forms and communities are present based on the potential natural communities present.
Native species	Most native aquatic species and life histories that would be expected based on potential natural communities are present and self-maintaining. Limited intermixing of native species genetics with outside sources has occurred, which can happen when moving aquatic species from one aquatic habitat to another.	Residual and, at times isolated, native endemic species that would be expected based on potential natural communities may be located in specific aquatic habitats. Some nonnative species may be present but native species are self-sustaining where found.	Exotic and/or aquatic invasive species are present and have mostly replaced native aquatic species. Legacy management effects to habitat from chemicals, sediment or other pollution may limit the knowledge available on endemic native species. Aquatic habitat is disconnected by passage or flow barriers.
Exotic and/or aquatic invasive species	Exotic and/or aquatic invasive species may be present but they have not greatly altered condition of native species (less than 25 percent of the historic aquatic-life-bearing habitats have exotic and/or aquatic invasive species present, spread of exotics and/or aquatic invasive species have been minimal over the past decade).	Exotic and/or aquatic invasive species are generally present and have lowered the health and sustainability of native species (between 25 and 50 percent of the historic native aquatic-life-bearing habitats have exotic and/or aquatic invasive species present and/or there has been an expansion of exotic and/or aquatic invasive species over the past decade).	Exotic and/or aquatic invasive species are present and have greatly lowered the condition of native aquatic species (more than 50 percent of the historic native-fish-bearing streams have exotic and/or aquatic invasive species present and/or there has been an expansion of nonnative exotic and/or aquatic invasive species over the past decade.

Additional Guidance

1. Life form presence. Avoid focus on single species; focus on communities.

2. Exotic and/or aquatic invasive species. The presence of exotic and/or aquatic invasive species or communities is used as an indicator of altered or impaired conditions. Although exotic and/or aquatic invasive species can significantly affect native aquatic faunal integrity, intraspecies interactions are not considered for this assessment. For this assessment, the widespread presence of exotic and/or aquatic invasive species indicates poor conditions. For example, if you note the presence of bluegill in an area that historically supported native rainbow trout, and you find in your records that water temperatures and flow conditions are now favoring bluegill and are not providing suitable habitat conditions for trout, your conclusion is that the habitat is in poor condition and the presence of bluegill is an indicator of this condition.

Definitions

aquatic invasive. Nonnative species that are also considered invasive.

exotic species. Nonnative species that are not considered invasive.

native fauna. Any faunal species native to a watershed.

Rationale for Indicator

Native fish and other native aquatic biota have been adversely affected by land and watershed development, habitat loss, direct human harvest, and increased competition from introduced exotic and/or aquatic invasive species. Introduced species and stocks are major threats to native fishes and aquatic biota by way of predation, competition, introduction of diseases and parasites for which native species lack resistance, environmental modification, inhibition of reproduction, and hybridization (Moyle et al. 1986, Nehlsen et al. 1991). Non-native introductions of species frequently have effects that cascade through entire ecosystems and compromise ecological structure and function in unforeseen ways (Winter and Hughes 1995). Although introductions have increased fishing opportunities, the ecological consequences have been high and the dramatic expansion of nonnative species has left many systems compromised (Angermeier and Karr 1994).

Indicator References

Angermeier, P.L.; Karr, J.R. 1994. Biological integrity versus biological diversity as policy directives: protecting biotic resources. BioScience. 44(10): 690–697.

Moyle, P.B.; Li, H.W.; Barton, B.A. 1986. The Frankenstein effect: impact of introduced fishes on native fishes in North America. In: Stroud, R.H., ed. Fish culture in fisheries management. Bethesda, MD: American Fisheries Society: 415–426.

Nehlsen, W.; Williams, J.E.; Lichatowich, J.A. 1991. Pacific salmon at the crossroads: stocks at risk from California, Oregon, Idaho, and Washington. Fisheries. 16: 4–21.

Winter, B.D.; Hughes, R.M. 1995. AFS draft position on biodiversity. Fisheries. 20(4): 20–25.

5. Riparian/Wetland Vegetation Condition

Purpose

This indicator addresses the function and condition of native riparian vegetation along streams, water bodies, and wetlands.

Condition Rating Rule Set

5. Riparian/ Wetland Vegetation Condition Indicator	Native vegetation is functioning properly throughout the stream corridor or along wetlands and water bodies.	Disturbance partially compromises the properly functioning condition of native vegetation attributes in stream corridor areas or along wetlands and water bodies.	A large percent of native vegetation attributes along stream corridors, wetlands, and water bodies is not functioning properly.
Attributes	**Good (1) Functioning Properly**	**Fair (2) Functioning at Risk**	**Poor (3) Impaired Function**
Vegetation condition	Native mid to late seral vegetation appropriate to the site's potential dominates the plant communities and is vigorous, healthy, and diverse in age, structure, cover, and composition on more than 80 percent of the riparian/wetland areas in the watershed. Sufficient reproduction of native species appropriate to the site is occurring to ensure sustainability. Mesic herbaceous plant communities occupy most of their site potential. Vegetation is in a dynamic equilibrium appropriate to the stream or wetland system.	Native vegetation demonstrates a moderate loss of vigor, reproduction, and growth, or it changes in composition, especially in areas most susceptible to human impact. Areas displaying light to moderate impact to structure, reproduction, composition, and cover may occupy 25 to 80 percent of the overall riparian area with only a few areas displaying significant impacts. Up to 25 percent of the species cover or composition occurs from early seral species and/or there exist some localized but relatively small areas where early seral vegetation dominates, but the communities across the watershed are still dominated by mid to late seral vegetation. Xeric herbaceous communities exist where water relationships have been altered but they are relatively small and localized, generally are not continuous across large areas, and do not dominate across the watershed.	Native vegetation is vigorous, healthy, and diverse in age, structure, cover, and composition on less than 25 percent of the riparian/wetland areas in the watershed. Native vegetation demonstrates a noticeable loss of vigor, reproduction, growth, and changes in composition as compared with the site's potential communities throughout areas most susceptible to human impact. In these areas, cover and composition are strongly reflective of early seral species dominance although late- and mid-seral species will be present, especially in pockets. Mesic-dependent herbaceous vegetation is limited in extent with many lower terraces dominated by xeric species most commonly associated with uplands. Reproduction of mid and late seral species is very limited. For much of the area, the water table is disconnected from the riparian area and the vegetation reflects this loss of available soil water.

Additional Guidance

1. Use the following riparian/wetland vegetation attribute questions to help you evaluate the existing condition of riparian/wetland vegetation in the watershed (Prichard et al. 1988). In all cases, evaluate the site relative to the site's potential natural vegetation:

   a. Is there a diverse age-class distribution of native riparian/wetland vegetation (recruitment for maintenance and recovery)?

   b. Is there a diverse composition of native riparian/wetland vegetation (for maintenance and recovery)?

   c. Are native species present that indicate maintenance of riparian/wetland soil moisture characteristics and connectivity between the riparian/wetland vegetation and the water table typical of riparian/wetland systems in the area?

   d. Is streambank native vegetation composed of those plants or plant communities that have root masses capable of withstanding high streamflow events?

   e. Does native riparian/wetland vegetative adequately cover and protect banks and dissipate energy during high flows?

   f. Do native riparian/wetland plants exhibit high vigor?

g. Are native plant communities an adequate source of coarse and/or large woody material (for maintenance and recovery)?

2. If forest plan riparian management direction exists for riparian/wetland vegetation, use the local thresholds derived from forest plan standards and guidelines to determine the appropriate rating for this attribute. For example, riparian timber stand conditions may be appropriate in some ecosystems as a measure of riparian vegetation condition but riparian/wetland herbaceous vegetation conditions are appropriate for other systems.

3. Where the Bureau of Land Management's Proper Functioning Condition assessments have been completed (Prichard et al. 1994), rate the properly functioning condition category as Condition Class 1, the functional at risk category as Condition Class 2, and the nonfunctional category as Condition Class 3 based on the percent of riparian areas in each category.

Definitions

functional at risk (functioning at risk). Riparian/wetland areas that are in functional condition, but one or more existing soil, water, or vegetation attributes makes them susceptible to degradation.

functioning properly. Riparian/wetland health (functioning condition), an important component of watershed condition, refers to the ecological status of vegetation, geomorphic, and hydrologic development, along with the degree of structural integrity exhibited by the riparian/wetland area. Riparian/wetland areas that are functioning properly exist when adequate vegetation, landform, or large woody debris is present to dissipate stream energy associated with high waterflow, thereby reducing erosion and improving water quality; filter sediment, capture bedload, and aid floodplain development; improve flood-water retention and ground-water recharge; develop root masses that stabilize streambanks against cutting action; develop diverse ponding and channel characteristics to provide the habitat and the water depth, duration, and temperature necessary for fish production, waterfowl breeding, and other uses; and support greater biodiversity.

nonfunctional (impaired). Riparian/wetland areas that clearly are not providing adequate vegetation, landform, or large woody debris to dissipate stream energy associated with high flows, and thus are not reducing erosion, improving water quality, etc.

riparian zone, riparian area, stream corridor. The interface between land and the banks of a stream, river, or other body of water. We use the term riparian in its broadest sense to include areas adjacent to a stream, river, or lake, recognizing that a diverse mixture of different definitions exists across the United States. Plant communities along these water margins are called riparian vegetation and are characterized by hydrophytic plants.

wetlands. Those areas that are inundated or saturated by surface or ground water at a frequency and duration sufficient to support, and that under normal circumstances do support, a prevalence of vegetation typically adapted for life in saturated soil conditions. In general, wetlands include swamps, marshes, bogs, and similar areas.

Rationale for Indicator

Riparian and wetland areas are the interface between terrestrial and aquatic ecosystems and are an integral part of the watersheds. Consequently, the health of these areas is closely interrelated to the condition of the surrounding watershed (Debano and Schmidt 1989, Hornbeck and Kochenderfer 2000). The health of riparian corridors is dependent on the storage and movement of sediment through the channel system and also on the movement of sediment and water from surrounding hillslopes into the channel system. Human-induced and natural disturbances can alter these processes either indirectly to the watershed or directly to riparian areas themselves by livestock grazing, road construction, mining, irrigation diversion, channel modification, flooding, wildfire, and similar disturbances (Baker et al. 2004, NRC 2002). One good measure of riparian/wetland health is the ecological condition of riparian vegetation relative to reference conditions.

Indicator References

Baker, M.B.; Ffolliott, P.F.; DeBano, L.F.; Neary, D.G., eds. 2004. Riparian areas of the Southwestern United States: hydrology, ecology and management. Boca Raton, FL: CRC Press.

DeBano, L.F.; Schmidt, L.J. 1989. Improving riparian areas through watershed management. Gen. Tech. Rep. RM-182. Fort Collins, CO: U.S. Department of Agriculture, Forest Service, Rocky Mountain Forest and Range Experiment Station.

Hornbeck, J.W.; Kochenderfer, J.N. 2000. Linkages between forests and streams: a perspective in time. In: Verry, E.S.; Hornbeck, J.W.; Dolloff, C.A., eds. Riparian management in forests of the continental Eastern United States. Boca Raton, FL: Lewis Publishers and CRC Press: 89–98.

National Research Council (NRC). 2002. Riparian areas: functions and strategies for management. Washington, DC: National Academy of Science.

Prichard, D.; Anderson, J.; Correll, C., et al. 1998. A user guide to assessing proper functioning condition and the supporting science for lotic areas. TR 1737-9. BLM/RS/ST-98/001+1737. Denver, CO: U.S. Department of the Interior, Bureau of Land Management, National Applied Resource Sciences Center. 126 p.

Prichard, D.; Bridges, C.; Krapf, R., et al. 1994. Riparian area management: process for assessing proper functioning condition for lentic riparian-wetland areas. TR 1737-11. BLM/SC/ST-94/008+1737. Denver, CO: U.S. Department of the Interior, Bureau of Land Management, Denver Service Center. 136 p.

6. Roads and Trails Condition

Purpose

This indicator addresses changes to the hydrologic and sediment regimes due to the density, location, distribution, and maintenance of the road and trail network.

Condition Rating Rule Set

6. Roads and Trails Condition Indicator	The density and distribution of roads and linear features within the watershed indicate that the hydrologic regime is substantially intact and unaltered.	The density and distribution of roads and linear features within the watershed indicates that there is a moderate probability that the hydrologic regime is substantially altered.	The density and distribution of roads and linear features within the watershed indicates that there is a higher probability that the hydrologic regime (timing, magnitude, duration, and spatial distribution of runoff flows) is substantially altered.
Attributes	**Good (1) Functioning Properly**	**Fair (2) Functioning at Risk**	**Poor (3) Impaired Function**
Open road density	Default road/trail density: less than 1 mi/mi^2, or a locally determined threshold for good conditions supported by forest plans or analysis and data.	Default road/trail density: From 1 to 2.4 mi/mi^2, or a locally determined threshold for fair conditions supported by forest plans or analysis and data.	Default road/trail density: more than 2.4 mi/mi^2, or a locally determined threshold for poor conditions supported by forest plans or analysis and data.
Road and trail maintenance	Best Management Practices (BMPs) for the maintenance of designed drainage features are applied to more than 75 percent of the roads, trails, and water crossings in the watershed.	BMPs for the maintenance of designed drainage features are applied to 50 to 75 percent of the roads, trails, and water crossings in the watershed.	BMPs for the maintenance of designed drainage features are applied to less than 50 percent of the roads, trails, and water crossings in the watershed.
Proximity to water	No more than 10 percent of road/trail length is located within 300 feet of streams and water bodies or hydrologically connected to them.	Between 10 and 25 percent of road/trail length is located within 300 feet of streams and water bodies or hydrologically connected to them.	More than 25 percent of road/trail length is located within 300 feet of streams and water bodies or hydrologically connected to them.
Mass wasting	Very few roads are on unstable landforms or rock types subject to mass wasting with little evidence of active movement or evidence of road damage. There is no danger of large quantities of debris being delivered to the stream channel because of mass wasting.	A few roads are on unstable landforms or rock types subject to mass wasting with moderate evidence of active movement or road damage. There is some danger of large quantities of debris being delivered to the stream channel, although this is not a primary concern in this watershed.	Most roads are on unstable landforms or rock types subject to mass wasting with extensive evidence of active movement or road damage. Mass wasting that could deliver large quantities of debris to the stream channel is a primary concern in this watershed.

Additional Guidance

1. For the purposes of this reconnaissance-level assessment, the term "road" is broadly defined to include roads and all lineal features on the landscape that typically influence watershed processes and conditions in a manner similar to roads. Roads, therefore, include Forest Service system roads (paved or nonpaved) and any temporary roads (skid trails, legacy roads) not closed or decommissioned, including private roads in these categories. Other linear features that might be included based on their prevalence or impact in a local area are motorized (off-road vehicle, all-terrain vehicle) and nonmotorized (recreational) trails and linear

features, such as railroads. Properly closed roads should be hydrologically disconnected from the stream network. If roads have a closure order but are still contributing to hydrological damage they should be considered open for the purposes of road density calculations.

2. Open road density. Although default road density guidelines (USFWS 1998) for good, fair, and poor conditions are provided, forests may deviate from the default values based on local analysis and/or forest plan standards and guidelines. For example, existing local or regional planning processes, publications, or other analyses may have established thresholds that are more pertinent to local conditions. The

selected default road density guidelines were derived from U.S. Fish and Wildlife Service guidance that covered a large geographical area of the Western United States.

3. Mass wasting. Mass movement is rated only with respect to the extent and effect it is associated with roads and effects to aquatic resources. Areas that are inherently unstable or at risk from mass movement are not rated.

4. Mass wasting. Geographical areas where mass wasting is not a significant process, may be rated as N/A. Typically, this designation would be applied over a broad geographic area such as an entire national forest. Coordination with the Regional Oversight Team is suggested to ensure consistency among adjacent units.

Definitions

hydrologically connected. Any road segment that, during a high runoff event, has a continuous surface flow path between the road prism and a natural stream channel is a hydrologically connected road segment. The proximity of roads to streams is a surrogate for hydrologic connectivity.

mass wasting. The geomorphic process by which soil, regolith, and rock move downslope under the force of gravity. Mass wasting may also be known as slope movement or mass movement. It encompasses a broad range of gravity-driven rock, soil, or sediment movements, including weathering processes. Types of mass wasting include creep, slides, flows, topples, and falls, and they are differentiated by how the soil, regolith, or rock moves downslope as a whole.

unstable landforms, geologic types, and landslide prone areas. Areas determined unstable by individual national forests using exiting soil resource inventories, terrestrial ecological unit inventories, geologic inventories, or maps.

Rationale for Indicator

Roads affect watershed condition because more sediment is contributed to streams from roads and road construction than any other land management activity. Roads directly alter natural sediment and hydrologic regimes by changing streamflow patterns and amounts, sediment loading, transport, deposition, channel morphology and stability, and water quality and riparian conditions within a watershed (Copstead et al. 1997, Dunne and Leopold 1978, Gibbons and Salo 1973). Road maintenance can also increase sediment routing to streams by creating areas prone to surface runoff, altering slope stability in cut-and-fill areas, removing vegetation, and altering drainage patterns

(Burroughs and King 1989, Luce and Black 2001, Megahan 1978, Reid and Dunne 1984). Road density is known to play a dominant role in human-induced augmentation of sediment supply by erosion and mass wasting in upland forested landscapes in the Pacific Northwest (Cederholm et al. 1981, Furniss et al. 1991), and it is reasonable to assume that similar relationships exist elsewhere. Road-related mass soil movements can continue for decades after roads have been constructed, and long-term slope failures frequently occur after road construction and timber harvest (Megahan and Bohn 1989).

Indicator References

Burroughs, E.R., Jr.; King, J.G. 1989. Reduction of soil erosion on forest roads. Gen. Tech. Rep. INT-264. U.S. Department of Agriculture, Forest Service, Intermountain Research Station. Ogden, UT. 21 p.

Cederholm, C.J.; Reid, L.M.; Salo, E.O. 1981. Cumulative effects of logging road sediment on salmonid populations of the Clearwater River, Jefferson County, Washington. In: Proceedings: Conference on salmon spawning gravel: a renewable resource in the Pacific Northwest? Report 19. Pullman, WA: Washington State University, Water Research Center: 38–74.

Copstead, R.; Moore, K.; Ledwith, T.; Furniss, M. 1997. Water/road interaction: an annotated bibliography. Water/Road Interaction Technology Series. Pub. 9777 1816P. Washington, DC: U.S. Department of Agriculture, Forest Service, Technology and Development Center. 162 p.

Dunne, T.; Leopold, L.B. 1978. Water in environmental planning. New York: W.H. Freeman. 818 p.

Furniss, M.J.; Roelofs, T.D.; Yee, C.S. 1991. Road construction and maintenance. In: Meehan, W.R., ed. Influences of forest and rangeland management. Special Publication 19. Bethesda, MD: American Fisheries Society: 297–324.

Gibbons, D.R.; Salo, E.O. 1973. An annotated bibliography of the effects of logging on fish of the Western United States and Canada. Gen. Tech. Rep. PNW-10. Portland, OR: U.S. Department of Agriculture, Forest Service, Pacific Northwest Forest and Range Experiment Station. 145 p.

Luce, C.H.; Black, T.A. 2001. Effects of traffic and ditch maintenance on forest road sediment production. In: Proceedings: seventh Federal interagency sedimentation conference: V67–V74.

Megahan, W.F. 1978. Erosion processes on steep granitic road fills in central Idaho. Soil Society of America Journal. 43(2): 350–357.

Megahan, W.F.; Bohn, C.C. 1989. Progressive, long-term slope failure following road construction and logging on noncohesive, granitic soils of the Idaho Batholith. In: Woessner, W.W.; Potts, D.F., eds. Proceedings: Symposium on headwaters hydrology, American Water Resources Association: 501–510.

Reid, L.M.; Dunne, T. 1984. Sediment production from forest road surfaces. Water Resources Research. 20: 1753–1761.

U.S. Fish and Wildlife Service (USFWS). 2000. A framework to assist in making Endangered Species Act determinations of effect for individual or grouped actions at the bull trout subpopulation watershed scale. In: Appendix 9 of the Interior Columbia Basin Ecosystem Management Project, Supplemental Draft Environmental Impact Statement. Boise, ID. USDA Forest Service and Bureau of Land Management. http://www.icbemp. gov/pdfs/sdeis/Volume2/Appendix9.pdf. (24 March 2011).

7. Soils Condition

Purpose

This indicator addresses alteration to natural soil condition, including productivity, erosion, and chemical contamination.

Condition Rating Rule Set

7. Soils Condition Indicator	Minor or no alteration to reference soil condition, including erosion, productivity, and chemical characteristics is evident.	Moderate amount of alteration to reference soil condition is evident. Overall soil disturbance is characterized as moderate.	Significant alteration to reference soil condition is evident. Overall soil disturbance is characterized as extensive.
Attributes	**Good (1) Functioning Properly**	**Fair (2) Functioning at Risk**	**Poor (3) Impaired Function**
Soil productivity	Soil nutrient and hydrologic cycling processes are functioning at near site-potential levels, and the ability of the soil to maintain resource values and sustain outputs is high in the majority of the watershed.	Soil nutrient and hydrologic cycling processes are impaired and the ability of the soil to maintain resource values and sustain outputs is compromised in 5 to 25 percent of the watershed.	Soil nutrient and hydrologic cycling processes are impaired and the ability of the soil to maintain resource values and sustain outputs is compromised in more than 25 percent of the watershed.
Soil erosion	Evidence of accelerated surface erosion is generally absent over the majority of the watershed.	Evidence of accelerated surface erosion occurs over less than 10 percent of the watershed, or rills and gullies are present but are generally small, disconnected, poorly defined, and not connected into any pattern.	Evidence of accelerated surface erosion occurs over more than 10 percent of the watershed, or rills and gullies are actively expanding, well-defined, continuous, and connected in a definite pattern.
Soil contamination	No substantial areas of soil contamination in the watershed exist. When atmospheric deposition is a source of contamination, sulfur and/or nitrogen deposition is more than 10 percent below the terrestrial critical load.	Limited areas of soil contamination may be present, but they do not have a substantial effect on overall soil quality. When atmospheric deposition is a source of contamination, sulfur and/or nitrogen deposition is 0 to 10 percent below the terrestrial critical load.	Extensive areas of soil contamination may be present. When atmospheric deposition is a source of contamination, sulfur and/or nitrogen deposition is above the terrestrial critical load.

Additional Guidance

1. If forest or regional direction exists for soil quality or soil management, these local thresholds may be used to determine the appropriate rating for soil attributes.

2. Soil nutrient and hydrologic cycling processes are evaluated using available relevant soil properties such as compaction, porosity, infiltration, bulk density, organic matter, soil cover, microbial activity, or other appropriate indicators.

3. Soil erosion should not double count road-related erosion effects that are considered in the roads and trails condition indicator.

4. Atmospheric deposition. Compare current deposition with either site-specific terrestrial critical loads for acidity and/or nutrient nitrogen (Geiser et al. 2010, Pardo et al. in review),

or with the best available critical loads calculated for similar sites in the region. Where acidification is the primary concern and site-specific critical loads are absent, use the risk assessment map of exceedence of critical loads (based on McNulty et al. 2007) to classify the watershed. Current information (including directions to Geographic Information System (GIS) coverage) for site-specific, regional, and national scale critical loads is available at http://www.fs.fed.us/air.

Definitions

critical load. The amount of deposition of an atmospheric pollutant below which no harmful ecological effects occur. We can calculate critical loads for both acidity and nutrient nitrogen in terrestrial and aquatic systems.

reference soil condition. The condition of the soil with which functional capacity is compared. Using indicators, soil quality is usually assessed by comparing a management system with a reference condition. The reference condition may be represented with (1) baseline measurements taken previously at the same location; (2) established and achievable indicator values such as salinity levels related to salt tolerance of crops; or (3) measurements from the same or similar soil under the reference state or inherent or attainable conditions (Tugel et al. 2008).

soil condition. A description of soil physical, chemical and biological properties that affect soil ecosystem services, including productivity, hydrologic function, stability, and resilience.

Rationale for Indicator

Determining natural soil condition includes evaluating erosion, nutrients, productivity, and the physical, chemical, and biological characteristics of the soil (USDA Forest Service 2009). Soil condition is related to watershed condition because of significant water supply benefits associated with developing forest soils that promote infiltration and high-quality water. Forest soils, with litter layers, high organic content, and large macropore fraction, promote rapid infiltration and minimize erosive overland flow (Ice 2009). In other ecosystems, soil supplies air, water, nutrients, and mechanical support for the sustenance of plants. It also receives and processes rainfall and controls how much of that rainfall becomes surface runoff, how much is stored for slow, sustained delivery to stream channels, and how much is stored and used for soil processes (Neary et al. 2005). Management activities, such as intensive grazing, logging, recreational activity, and other disturbances, can lead to reduced soil structure, soil compaction, and damage to or loss of vegetative cover. These activities contribute to increased surface runoff resulting in soil erosion, loss of nutrients, and a decrease in soil productivity (Meehan and Platts 1978). The soil contamination attribute addresses various sources of contaminants, including abandoned mines, illegal dumping, drug labs, spills, atmospheric deposition, and others. For atmospheric sources, the critical load standard addresses the impact of air pollution (sulfur and nitrogen) deposition on forest soils. Sulfur and/or nitrogen deposition estimates above the critical load for soil indicate the potential for significant harmful effects to the forest ecosystem through the accelerated loss of base cations, a decrease in soil pH, an increased risk of biologically toxic levels of aluminum released from the soils, or nitrogen in excess of and detrimental to biological demand.

Indicator References

Geiser, L.G.; Jovan, S.E.; Glavich, D.A.; Porter, M.K. 2010. Lichen-based critical loads for atmospheric deposition in Western Oregon and Washington forests, USA. Environmental Pollution. 158: 2412–2421.

Ice, G.G. 2009. Comments on using forestry to secure America's water supply. Journal of Forestry. 107(3): 150.

McNulty, S.G.; Cohen, E.C.; Moore Myers, J.A., et al. 2007. Estimates of critical acid loads and exceedances for forest soils across the conterminous United States. Environmental Pollution. 149: 281–292.

Meehan, W.P.; Platts, W.S. 1978. Livestock grazing and the aquatic environment. Journal of Soil and Water Conservation. 33(6): 274–278.

Neary, D.G.; Ryan, K.C.; DeBano, L.F., eds. 2005. Wildland fire in ecosystems: effects of fire on soils and water. Gen. Tech. Rep. RMRS-GTR-42-vol.4. Ogden, UT: U.S. Department of Agriculture, Forest Service, Rocky Mountain Research Station. 250 p.

Pardo, L.H.; Geiser, L.H.; Goodale, C.L., et al. In review. Assessment of effects of N deposition and empirical critical loads for nitrogen for ecoregions of the United States. Gen. Tech. Rep. Washington, DC: U.S. Department of Agriculture, Forest Service. 200 p.

Tugel, A.J.; Skye, A.W.; Herrick, J.E. 2008. Soil change guide: procedures for soil survey and resource inventory. Lincoln, NE: U.S. Department of Agriculture, Natural Resources Conservation Service, National Soil Survey Center. Ver. 1.1.

U.S. Department of Agriculture (USDA), Forest Service. 2009. Soil management manual. FSM 2550. Washington, DC: U.S. Department of Agriculture, Forest Service. 9 p.

8. Fire Regime or Wildfire Condition

Purpose

This indicator addresses the potential for altered hydrologic and sediment regimes because of departures from historical ranges of variability in vegetation, fuel composition, fire frequency, fire severity, and fire pattern.

Condition Rating Rule Set

8. Fire Regime or Wildfire Condition Indicator	Low likelihood of losing defining ecosystem components because of the presence or absence of fire.	Moderate likelihood of losing defining ecosystem components because of the presence or absence of fire.	High likelihood of losing defining ecosystem components because of the presence or absence of fire.
Attributes	**Good (1) Functioning Properly**	**Fair (2) Functioning at Risk**	**Poor (3) Impaired Function**
Fire Regime Condition Class	Fire Regime Condition Class (FRCC) 1—A predominate percentage of the watershed is within the natural (historical) range of variability ("reference fire regime") of vegetation characteristics; fuel composition; fire frequency, severity, and pattern; and other associated disturbances. The vegetative species and cover types are well adapted to the fire regime and offer good protection to soil and water resources.	FRCC 2—A predominate percentage of the watershed has a moderate departure from the reference fire regime of vegetation characteristics; fuel composition; fire frequency, severity, and pattern; and other associated disturbances. The vegetative species and cover types are somewhat affected by the abnormal fire regime and this results in less protection to soil and water resources when fire occurs.	FRCC 3—A predominate percentage of the watershed has a high departure from the reference fire regime of vegetation characteristics; fuel composition; fire frequency, severity, and pattern; and other associated disturbances. The vegetative species and cover types are affected by the fire regime and this results in periods of fuel accumulation with infrequent intense fires with high severity that are more likely to lead to vegetation mortality, loss of soil organic matter, and poor protection to soil and water resources.
Attributes	**Good (1) Functioning Properly**	**Fair (2) Functioning at Risk**	**Poor (3) Impaired Function**
Wildfire Effects	Following a significant wildfire, effects are such that soil and ground cover conditions in the burned area are expected to recover within 1 to 2 years to levels that provide watershed protection appropriate for the location and ecotype.	Following a significant wildfire, soil and ground cover conditions are causing some post-fire runoff and erosion concerns but are not sufficient to jeopardize long-term watershed condition integrity. This condition may persist for 2 to 5 years after a wildfire.	Following a significant wildfire, soil and ground cover conditions are causing considerable post-fire runoff, erosion, and flooding threats to watershed condition integrity lasting for more than 5 years.

Additional Guidance

1. The Fire Regime or Wildfire Condition Indicator is unique in that it is an either/or proposition in which either Fire Regime Condition or Wildfire Effects is rated. In most cases, we will rate the Fire Regime attribute. Following a significant wildfire, however, the Wildfire Effects attribute is rated and the Fire Regime attribute is rated N/A. This is the only indicator that operates in this either/or manner.

2. Wildfire Effects. We will rate watersheds experiencing a significant wildfire (one that effectively changes the FRCC using the Wildfire Effects attribute until the watershed fully recovers from any adverse wildfire effects (i.e., recovers from a rating of 2 or 3), and during this time we will rate the FRCC attribute as N/A. Forests should switch to the Wildfire Effects attribute if more than 50 percent of the watershed is affected by a significant wildfire. If less than 50 percent of the watershed is affected by a significant wildfire, switching to this attribute may still be appropriate and should be determined by the forest on a case-by-case basis. In the wake of a significant wildfire, only the Wildfire Effects attribute correctly characterizes the state of the watershed with respect to watershed condition. For example, following a severe wildfire, a watershed previously in

FRCC3 (Poor) reverts to FRCC1 (Good) because it has been returned to its natural reference condition and the Wildfire Effects attribute will now be rated as 3 (Poor) due to post-fire conditions. Averaging the two attributes will result in an incorrect characterization of watershed condition. To avoid this, we will rate watershed condition based on the Wildfire Effects attribute during the entire watershed recovery period.

3. Fire Regime Condition Class. In watersheds that clearly have more than one FRCC, use the formula below to determine the Category.

Methodology:

a. For each 6th-level hydrologic unit code (HUC) watershed, determine the percentage of the total watershed area within each of the Fire Regime Condition Classes (FRCC1, FRCC2, and FRCC3). Use GIS overlays if possible.

b. FRCC1 is assigned a category score of 1, FRCC2 is assigned a category score of 2, and FRCC3 is assigned a category score of 3.

c. Calculate the weighted average fire regime condition class (FRCC$_{wtavg}$) using the formula below:

$$FRCC_{wtavg} = \frac{(FRCC1*1)+(FRCC2*2)+(FRCC3*3)}{FRCC1+FRCC2+FRCC3}$$

where:

FRCC1 = acres of watershed within Fire Regime Condition Class 1,

FRCC2 = acres of watershed within Fire Regime Condition Class 2,

FRCC3 = acres of watershed within Fire Regime Condition Class 3.

Categorize fire regime condition using the following calculated weighted average FRCC ranges:

Category 1—1.0 to 1.66.

Category 2—1.67 to 2.33.

Category 3—2.33 to 3.0.

4. Fire Regime Condition Class. Although the use of national FRCC map products is encouraged, forests may refine FRCC as appropriate to fit their local situations.

a. Example 1. Forests in the Southern Region may wish to use the Fire Frequency-Severity Condition Class

and omit the Succession Class Condition Class in their determination of Watershed Condition ratings since this seems more appropriate for these ecosystems.

b. Example 2. Forests in the Southwest may wish to use Integrated Forest Resource Management System (INFORMS) data instead of the national Landscape Fire and Resource Management Planning Tools (LANDFIRE) data since it provides a better estimate of local conditions.

Document and coordinate modifications with your Regional Oversight Team.

Definitions

Fire Regime Condition Class (FRCC). Fire regime condition classes measure the degree of departure from reference conditions, possibly resulting in changes to key ecosystem components, such as vegetation characteristics (species composition, structural stage, stand age, canopy closure, and mosaic pattern); fuel composition; fire frequency, severity, and pattern; and other associated disturbances, such as insect and disease mortality, grazing, and drought. Possible causes of this departure include (but are not limited to) fire suppression, timber harvesting, livestock grazing, introduction and establishment of exotic plant species, and introduced insects and disease. FRCC is strictly a measure of ecological trends.

The three fire regime condition classes are categorized using the following criteria: FRCC1 represents ecosystems with low (less than 33 percent) departure and that are still within the estimated historical range of variability during a specifically defined reference period; FRCC2 indicates ecosystems with moderate (33 to 66 percent) departure; and FRCC 3 indicates ecosystems with high (more than 66 percent) departure from reference conditions. As described below, departure is based on a central tendency (or mean) metric and represents a composite estimate of the reference condition vegetation characteristics; fuel composition; fire frequency, severity, and pattern; and other associated natural disturbances. Low departure includes a range of plus or minus 33 percent deviation from the central tendency.

Characteristic vegetation and fuel conditions are considered to be those that occurred within the natural fire regime, such as those found in areas categorized as FRCC1 (low departure). Uncharacteristic conditions are considered to be those that did not occur within the natural regime, such as areas that are often categorized as FRCC2 and FRCC3 (moderate to high departure). These uncharacteristic conditions include, but are not limited to the following: invasive species (weeds and insects), diseases, "high graded" forest composition and structure (in which, for example, large, fire-tolerant trees have been removed and small fire-intolerant trees have been left within a frequent surface fire regime), or overgrazing by domestic livestock that adversely effects native grasslands or promotes unnatural levels of soil erosion (Hann et al. 2004, 2008).

watershed recovery period. The period of time, in years, that is required for the burned area to develop vegetation and infiltration conditions sufficient to reduce runoff and erosion potential to essentially predisturbance conditions. This is a best estimate of natural regeneration, soil stabilization, and hydrophobicity reduction, supplemented by any treatments prescribed (USDA Forest Service 2009).

Rationale for Indicator

To a large extent, watershed condition is controlled by the composition and density of vegetative cover and the amount of bare soil resulting from anthropogenic or natural disturbances that affect the watershed (Neary et al. 2005). Fire primarily alters vegetation and soil properties, changing hydrologic and geomorphic processes. In general, the effects of fire are increased soil water and overland flow that result in accelerated erosion by a variety of surface and mass movement processes. The magnitude of the effects on an ecosystem depends to a large degree on the frequency and intensity of fire and the sensitivity of the ecosystem to disturbance (Swanson 1981). Fire regime and geomorphic sensitivity may be used to characterize and contrast the geomorphic consequences of fire in different ecosystems. For example, frequent, intense fire in highly erosive landscapes, such as steep-land chaparral in southern California, is an extremely important component of some geomorphic systems. The effects of fire are progressively less significant in ecosystems in which fire is less frequent and/or less intense. FRCC, which is a measure of vegetation departure from reference condition, effectively evaluates potential vegetation change effects to watershed condition. Wildfires have the potential to exert a tremendous influence on the hydrologic conditions of watersheds in many forest ecosystems depending on the fire's severity, duration, and frequency. Wildfire is

the single forest disturbance that has the greatest potential to change watershed condition (DeBano et al. 1998). An extensive, high-severity wildfire can destroy the vegetation and litter layer in a watershed and detrimentally alter physical properties of the soil, including infiltration and percolation capacities. These cumulative fire effects can change the watershed condition from good to poor, resulting in unacceptable increases to overland flow, erosion, and soil loss (Neary et al. 2005).

Indicator References

DeBano, L.F.; Neary, D.G.; Ffolliott, P.F. 1998. Fire's effects on ecosystems. New York: John Wiley & Sons. 333 p.

Hann, W.; Shlisky, A.; Havlina, D., et al. 2004. Interagency fire regime condition class guidebook. Last update January 2008: Version 1.3.0 [Homepage of the Interagency and The Nature Conservancy Fire Regime Condition Class Web site, U.S. Department of Agriculture Forest Service, U.S. Department of the Interior, The Nature Conservancy, and Systems for Environmental Management]. http://www.frcc.gov.

Hann et al. 2008. Interagency and The Nature Conservancy Fire Regime Condition Class Web site. U.S. Department of Agriculture Forest Service, U.S. Department of the Interior, The Nature Conservancy, and Systems for Environmental Management. www.frcc.gov.

Neary, D.G.; Ryan, K.C.; DeBano, L.F., eds. 2005 (revised 2008). Wildland fire in ecosystems: effects of fire on soils and water. Gen. Tech. Rep. RMRS-GTR-42-Vol.4. Ogden, UT: U.S. Department of Agriculture, Forest Service, Rocky Mountain Research Station. 250 p.

Swanson, F.J. 1981. Fire and geomorphic processes. In: Mooney, H.A., et al., tech. coords. Fire regimes and ecosystem properties. Gen. Tech. Rep. WO-26. Washington, DC: U.S. Department of Agriculture, Forest Service: 410–420.

U.S. Department of Agriculture (USDA), Forest Service. 2009. Emergency stabilization, Burned-Area Emergency Response (BAER). FSM 2523. Washington, DC: U.S. Department of Agriculture, Forest Service.

9. Forest Cover Condition

Purpose

This indicator addresses the potential for altered hydrologic and sediment regimes because of the loss of forest cover on forest lands.

Condition Rating Rule Set

9. Forest Cover Condition Indicator	The amount of National Forest System (NFS) forest land in the watershed that is not supporting forest cover is minor.	The amount of NFS forest land in the watershed that is not supporting forest cover is moderate.	The amount of NFS forest land in the watershed that is not supporting forest cover is high.
Attributes	**Good (1) Functioning Properly**	**Fair (2) Functioning at Risk**	**Poor (3) Impaired Function**
Loss of forest cover	Less than 5 percent of NFS land in the watershed contains cut-over, denuded, or deforested forest land where appropriate forest cover should be reestablished or restored to achieve the desired conditions or other applicable forest plan direction for NFS lands.	Between 5 and 15 percent of NFS land in the watershed contains cut-over, denuded, or deforested forest land where appropriate forest cover should be reestablished or restored to achieve the desired conditions or other applicable forest plan direction for NFS lands.	More than 15 percent of NFS land in the watershed contains cut-over, denuded, or deforested forest land where appropriate forest cover should be reestablished or restored to achieve the desired conditions or other applicable forest plan direction for NFS lands.

Additional Guidance

1. This indicator focuses on the presence or absence of forest cover (lands being managed as natural or seminatural forest ecosystems) on NFS lands in consideration of National Forest Management Act (NFMA) requirements. Because non-NFS lands do not have this Federal legal standard for forest cover, those private and other ownerships are not included in rating the watershed for this indicator.

2. This indicator may be rated N/A if forest cover (as precisely defined below) is absent in the watershed. If forest cover is rated N/A, rangeland condition must be rated. In effect, we characterize a watershed as having forest cover, rangelands, or both. In many watersheds, we will rate both indicators. Note that lands that meet the forest land definition will also normally have a rangeland component to the understory. This is especially true in those forest lands where the tree cover is relatively sparse (normally less than 60 percent canopy cover), with the amount of rangeland vegetation increasing as tree canopy cover decreases. In these instances, both indicators shall be evaluated and rated.

3. We will produce the most accurate and rapid assessment if the Forest Service Activity Tracking System (FACTS) database reflects current conditions regarding loss of forest cover and planned or subsequent reforestation activities. Use sources such as Rapid Assessment of Vegetation Condition After Wildfire to update FACTS until field exams can be conducted. Apply FACTS business rules.

4. Methodology:

   a. Calculate percent for each 6th-level HUC watershed using the formula below:

   $$\frac{A_D}{A_T}\ (100)$$

   where:

   A_D = area (in acres) of NFS forest land within the watershed that is not providing forest cover. NFS forest land must meet all three of the following criteria:

   i. is being managed as forest land (a land-use determination defined by the land and resources management plan).

   ii. has been cut over, denuded, or lost forest cover from any human or natural disturbance.

   iii. where forest cover has not yet been reestablished. See the definition of "forest cover" below.

   A_T = total area (in acres) of NFS forest land within the watershed. Obtain from best source such as NRM-Natural Resource Information Systems (NRIS), legacy databases, other assessments, remote sensing, or GIS sources.

b. Using the percentage determined from step a, categorize each watershed's forest cover condition into either Category 1, 2, or 3.

Definitions

forest cover. Areas where trees provide 10 percent or greater canopy cover and are part of the dominant (uppermost) vegetation layer, including areas that have been planted to produce woody crops. For the purposes of watershed condition assessment, lands that do not yet provide 10 percent tree canopy cover will be considered as meeting the definition of forest cover if the areas have been certified and recorded in FACTS as having been regenerated to appropriate forest cover (whether through natural or artificial regeneration) as specified in the land and resources management plan. "Appropriate forest cover" may be defined in one or more of the following forest plan components (desired conditions, standards, guidelines, management area prescriptions and allocation map, map of lands suitable for timber production, or other direction). The following FACTS codes are applicable (these are used to generate the Reforestation Needs Report): Harvest Codes 4101, 4102, 4110-17, 4131-34, 4143, 4147, 4150-52, 4160, 4162, 4175-77, 4183, and 4194; Causal Agent: 4250, 4260, 4265, 4270, 4280, and 4290.

forest land. Land is at least 10 percent occupied by forest trees, or it previously had such tree cover, is and not currently developed for nonforest use. Lands developed for nonforest use include areas for crops, improved pasture, residential, or administrative areas, improved roads of any width, and adjoining road clearing and power-line clearing of any width (FSM 1905). Note: Designated wilderness, roadless areas, and unproductive forest land that meet the above definition are classified as forest land.

Rationale for Indicator

This is a foundational indicator of whether forest ecosystems are being sustained or lost over time ("Maintain forests as forests"). The ability of forests to regulate water flows and maintain quality supplies is affected by the condition of the forest and the occurrence of disturbances that change the structure, composition, and pattern of forest vegetation. Forest cover is a primary terrestrial ecosystem component that is important to watershed condition. Trees provide many water- and soil-related ecosystem services such as intercepting precipitation and protecting soil, regulating snowmelt, and stabilizing steep slopes. Extensive loss of forest cover because of severe wild-fires, widespread insect and disease epidemics, timber harvest, weather events, and long-term drought affect runoff, erosion, sediment supply, bank stability, large woody debris retention, and stream temperature relationships (MacDonald et al. 1991, Meehan 1991, Reid 1993). Many of the effects from these and similar disturbances decrease after the initial disturbance but may remain above natural levels for many years (Platts and Megahan 1975). Carefully designed and executed management actions can both restore vegetative cover and improve watershed condition.

Section 4 (Reforestation) of the Forest and Rangeland Renewable Resources Planning Act of 1974, as amended by NFMA (National Forest Management Act of 1976) (16 U.S.C. 1601(d) (1)), establishes the policy of Congress that all forested lands in the NFS be maintained in appropriate forest cover with species of trees, degree of stocking, rate of growth, and conditions of stand designed to secure the maximum benefits of multiple-use sustained yield management in accordance with land management plans.

Regarding private lands, note that some States (such as California) have forest regulations requiring reestablishment or maintenance of forest cover after timber harvest.

Indicator References

MacDonald, L.H.; Smart, A.; Wissmar, R.C. 1991. Monitoring guidelines to evaluate effects of forestry activities on streams in the Pacific Northwest and Alaska. EPA/910/9-91-001. Seattle, WA: U.S. Environmental Protection Agency, Region 10. 166 p.

Meehan, W.R., ed. 1991. Influences of forest and rangeland management on salmonid fishes and their habitat. Special Publication 19. Bethesda, MD: American Fisheries Society.

Platts, W.S.; Megahan, W.F. 1975. Time trends in riverbed sediment composition in salmon and steelhead spawning areas. In: Proceedings, 40th American wildlife and natural resources conference: 229–239.

Reid, L.M. 1993. Research and cumulative watershed effects. Gen. Tech. Rep. PSW-GTR-141. Albany, CA: U.S. Department of Agriculture, Forest Service, Pacific Southwest Research Station. 118 p.

U.S. Government. 1974. Forest and Rangeland Renewable Resources Planning Act of 1974, as amended by the National Forest Management Act of 1976 (16 United States Code 1600-1614, 472a).

10. Rangeland Vegetation Condition

Purpose

This indicator addresses impacts to soil and water relative to the vegetative health of rangelands.

Condition Rating Rule Set

10. Rangeland Vegetation Condition Indicator	Rangelands reflect native or desired nonnative plant composition and cover at near-natural levels as defined by the site potential.	Rangelands reflect native or desired nonnative plant composition and cover with slight to moderate deviation compared to natural levels as defined by the site potential.	Rangelands reflect native or desired nonnative plant composition and cover are greatly reduced or unacceptably altered compared to natural levels as defined by the site potential.
Attributes	**Good (1) Functioning Properly**	**Fair (2) Functioning at Risk**	**Poor (3) Impaired Function**
Rangeland vegetation condition	Vegetation contributes to soil condition, nutrient cycling, and hydrologic regimes at near-natural levels; functional/structural groups, number of species, plant mortality and decadence closely match that expected for the site average annual plant production equals or exceeds 70 percent of production potential; litter amount is approximately what is expected for the site potential and weather; the reproductive capacity of native or naturalized perennial plants to produce seeds or vegetative tillers is sustainable over the long term; and introduced plant species are being managed to facilitate long-term replacement by site-adapted native species.	Functional/structural groups and number of species are slightly to moderately reduced; some dead and/or decadent plants are present above what would be expected for the site; average annual plant production is 40 to 69 percent of production potential; litter amount is moderately less than would be expected relative to site potential and weather; the reproductive capacity of perennial native or naturalized plants to produce seeds or vegetative tillers is somewhat reduced but is still sustainable over the long term; and, introduced plant species are being managed to facilitate long-term replacement by site-adapted native species or to ensure adequate ground cover to protect the soil.	Functional/structural groups and number of species are moderately to greatly reduced or altered relative to site potential; dead and/or decadent plants are significantly more common than would be expected for the site; average annual plant production is less than 40 percent of production potential; litter is largely absent or is sparse and disconnected relative to site potential and weather; the reproductive capacity of native or naturalized perennial plants to produce seeds or vegetative tillers (native or seeded) is severely reduced relative to site potentials; and introduced plant species are dominant and are not effective in protecting the site and soil.

Additional Guidance

1. Rangelands are rated relative to biotic integrity. Use guidance and definitions found in the publication, "Interpreting Indicators of Rangeland Health" (Pellant et al. 2005), to assist with this evaluation. Because of the close interrelationship between soils, hydrology, and vegetation condition, rangeland ecologists, hydrologists, and soil scientists are encouraged to work together to make this evaluation. Rangeland soil/ and site stability and hydrologic function are rated in the Soils Condition indicator. Invasive species are rated in the Terrestrial Invasive Species Condition Indicator.

2. If forest plan rangeland direction exists for ecological condition (functional structural groups, plant mortality and decadence, annual production, litter amounts, reproductive capacity, or similar attributes), use the local thresholds derived from forest plan standards and guidelines to determine the appropriate rating.

3. This indicator may be rated N/A if rangelands (as defined below) are absent in the watershed. If rangeland is rated N/A, forest cover condition must be rated. In effect, we characterize a watershed as having forest cover, rangelands, or both. In many watersheds, we will rate both indicators. If rangelands are not present, we may decide to exclude them on an individual watershed basis, but in many cases the decision will apply to an entire national forest. Coordination with the Regional Oversight Team is recommended.

Definitions

biotic integrity (integrity of the biotic community). Capacity of a site to support characteristic functional and structural communities in the context of normal variability, to resist loss of this function and structure because of a disturbance, and to recover following such disturbance (Pellant et al. 2005).

functioning at risk. Rangelands that have a reversible loss in productive capability and increased vulnerability to irreversible degradation based upon an evaluation of current conditions of the soil and ecological processes (National Research Council 1994).

functioning properly. Rangelands that are functioning properly relative to the ecological site description and/or ecological reference area given the normal range of variability associated with the site and climate.

impaired. Rangelands on which degradation has resulted in the loss of ecological processes that function properly and the capacity to provide values and commodities to a degree that external inputs are required to restore the health of the land (National Research Council 1994).

rangeland. Land on which the indigenous vegetation (climax or natural potential) is predominantly grasses, grass-like plants, forbs, or shrubs and is managed as a natural ecosystem. If plants are introduced, they are managed similarly. Rangelands include natural grasslands, savannas, shrub lands, many deserts, tundra, alpine communities, marshes, and wet meadows (Society of Range Management 1999). (Pellant et al. 2005) include oak and pinyon-juniper woodlands in this definition). In this assessment, we will rate the condition of marshes under the Riparian/Wetland Vegetation indicator.

Rationale for Indicator

Rangeland health is a function of (1) soil/site stability—the capacity of the site to limit redistribution and loss of soil resources (including nutrients and organic matter) by wind and water; (2) hydrologic function—the capacity of the site to capture, store, and safely release water from rainfall, runoff, and snowmelt and to recover following disturbance; and (3) the integrity of the biotic community—the capacity of the site to support ecological processes within the normal range of variability expected for the site and to recover after a disturbance (Pellant et al. 2005). Improper management can decrease ground cover and reduce species diversity, composition and/or cover. Improper management can result in diminished watershed functionality through soil compaction, which may

increase overland flow and lead to incised channels and bank erosion (Bohn and Buckhouse 1986, Kaufman and Kreuger 1984, Platts 1991). Conversely, proper management can lessen adverse effects (Clary and Webster 1989). In summary, rangeland vegetative communities that are functioning properly provide for conditions that sustain soil stability, hydrologic function, and biotic diversity.

Indicator References

Bohn, C.C.; Buckhouse, J.C. 1986. Effects of grazing management on streambanks. Proceedings: North American wildlife natural resource conference. 51: 265–271.

Clary, W.P.; Webster, B.F. 1989. Managing grazing of riparian areas in the Intermountain Region. Gen. Tech. Rep. INT-263. Ogden, UT: U.S. Department of Agriculture, Forest Service, Intermountain Research Station. 11 p.

Johnson, K.L. 1992. Management for water quality on rangeland through best management practices: the Idaho approach. In: Watershed management: balancing sustainability and environmental change. New York: Springer-Verlag: 415–441.

Kaufmann, J.B.; Kreuger, W.C. 1984. Livestock impacts on riparian ecosystems and streamside management implications: a review. Journal of Range Management. 37: 430–438.

National Research Council. 1994. Rangeland health: new methods to classify, inventory, and monitor rangelands. Washington, DC: National Academy Press, National Research Council. 180 p.

Pellant, M.; Shaver, P.; Pyke, D.A.; Herrick, J.E. 2005. Interpreting indicators of rangeland health. Tech. Ref. 1734-6. BLM/WO/ST-00/001+1734/REV05. Denver, CO: U.S. Department of the Interior, Bureau of Land Management, National Science and Technology Center. 122 pp. Ver. 4. http://www.blm.gov/nstc/library/pdf/1734-6rev05.pdf. (24 March 2011).

Platts, W.S. 1991. Livestock grazing. In: Influence of forest and rangeland management on salmonid fishes and their habitats. Special Publication 19. Bethesda, MD: American Fisheries Society: 389–423.

Society for Range Management. 1999. A glossary of terms used in range management. Denver, CO: Society for Range Management. 20 p.

11. Terrestrial Invasive Species Condition

Purpose

This indicator addresses potential impacts to soil, vegetation, and water resources due to terrestrial invasive species (including vertebrates, invertebrates, and plants).

Condition Rating Rule Set

11. Terrestrial Invasive Species Condition Indicator	Few or no populations of terrestrial invasive species infest the watershed that could necessitate removal treatments that would affect soil and water resources.	Populations of terrestrial invasive species are established within the watersheds and/or the rate of expansion and/or potential for impact on watershed resources is moderate.	Terrestrial invasive species populations infest significant portions of the watershed, are expanding their range, and there is documentation of widespread impacts to watershed resources.
Attributes	**Good (1) Functioning Properly**	**Fair (2) Functioning at Risk**	**Poor (3) Impaired Function**
Extent and rate of spread	Few (less than 10 percent) or no populations of terrestrial invasive species infest the watershed that could necessitate removal treatments to protect, soil, native vegetation, or other water resources. Those that occur are small in extent and scattered in nature. The rate of spread and/ or potential for impact on watershed resources is minimal or unlikely. Management intervention may be necessary to prevent increased risk of spread or invasion. Integrated management treatments may temporarily negatively affect soil, native vegetation, and other water resources, but the scale and scope would be minor.	Populations of terrestrial invasive species are established within (10 to 25 percent) the watershed and/or the rate of spread and/or potential for impact on soil, vegetation, or other water resources is moderate. Integrated treatments affect 10 to 25 percent of the watershed and must be ongoing just to keep the invasive species in check. Management intervention will be required to prevent increased level of risk.	Populations of terrestrial invasive species infest significant portions (more than 25 percent) of the watershed, may be expanding their range, and widespread impacts to soil, native vegetation, or other water resources have been documented. Treatments for containment affect more than 25 percent of the watershed, and management adjustments and/or treatments need to be ongoing just to keep the invasive species in check. Management intervention is necessary to alleviate significant resource damage and increased degradation of watershed condition.

Additional Guidance

1. This indictor applies only to terrestrial vertebrates, invertebrates, and plants that may have an adverse effect on soil and water resources. Aquatic invasive species are considered under Aquatic Biota Condition. Invasive insects and pathogens (including native forest insect pests and diseases) are covered under the Forest Health indicator.

2. Infestation extent. Infestation extent is usually evaluated with risk assessments and other inventory and evaluation procedures at either the species level, site level, or project level. For example, the extent of the terrestrial invasive species infestation on an individual species-level may indicate that the watershed condition rating is "good," but when viewed within the context of all the documented terrestrial invasive species infesting the entire watershed, the overall condition rating may be considered "poor."

3. Integrated management treatments against terrestrial invasive species may temporarily negatively affect soil, native vegetation, and other watershed resources, requiring a restoration component to the project plan.

Definitions

native species. With respect to a particular ecosystem, a species that historically occurred in that ecosystem.

terrestrial invasive species. A terrestrial invasive species (including vertebrates, invertebrates, pathogens, and plants) is a species not native to the ecosystem location under consideration, and its introduction causes or is likely to cause economic or environmental harm, or harm to human health. The lack of natural ecological controls (which typically kept these exotic species regulated in their native home) allows these exotic species to significantly harm the areas they invade. Terrestrial invasive species refers to harmful exotic species that are found or occur on the land surface rather than in aquatic environments. Many exotic plant and animal species occupy terrestrial habitats, but they are not necessarily harmful and typically cause little to no economic or environmental damage, and do not out-compete or displace native plants or animals.

Rationale for Indicator

When they produce significant changes in ecological processes, invasive species may cause environmental harm to watershed conditions, sometimes across broad geographical areas, which results in conditions that native animal and plant communities cannot tolerate. Some invasive species can significantly alter effective ground cover, erosion rates, and nutrient cycling; change the frequency and intensity of wildfires; or alter the hydrology of rivers, streams, lakes, and wetlands (Mack et al. 2000). For example, for cheatgrass the link to soil and hydrologic processes is through a chain of logic that recognizes that while cheatgrass may seasonally provide adequate cover for watershed protection, because it is an annual that it leaves little to no vegetative soil protection in dry years to provide soil protection. Consequently, its overall ability to protect the soil is minimal (and is well outside of the native site potential). Also, since disturbance of the soil is the main reason cheatgrass spreads, it is closely associated with an undesirable condition from a soil and water perspective. Cheatgrass in the Great Basin region has been shown to decrease the interval between the occurrences of wildfires from once every 70 to 100 years to every 3 to 5 years because it forms dense stands of fine fuel annually. This decrease in interval between wildfires causes more severe soil erosion and dramatically alters desirable native plant communities (Knapp 1996; Pimentel et al. 2000). Similarly, tamarisk (salt cedar) [Tamarix spp.] in the Southwest disrupts the structure and stability of North American native riparian plant communities by out-competing and replacing native plant species, increasing soil salinity, monopolizing limited sources of moisture, and increasing the frequency, intensity, and effect of fires and floods. Tamarisk has taken over large sections of riparian ecosystems in the Western United States that were once home to native cottonwoods and willows (Christensen 1962; Stromberg 1998). In addition, infestations of terrestrial invasive vertebrate species such as wild (feral) pigs cause widespread soil erosion, harbor infectious diseases, damage native vegetation, and aggressively prey upon native vertebrate and invertebrate wildlife (USDA-APHIS 1999).

Indicator References

Christensen, E.M. 1962. The rate of naturalization of Tamarix in Utah. American Midland Naturalist. 68(1): 51–57.

Knapp, P.A. 1996. Cheatgrass (Bromus tectorum L.) dominance in the Great Basin Desert: history, persistence, and influences to human activities. Global Environmental Change. 6(1): 37–52.

Mack, R.; Simberloff, D.W.M.; Lonsdale, H., et al. 2000. Biotic invasions: causes, epidemiology, global consequences, and control. Ecological Applications. 10: 689–710.

Pimentel, D.; Lach, L.; Zuniga, R.; Morrison, D. 2000. Environmental and economic costs of nonindigenous species in the United States. Bioscience. 50(1): 53–65.

Stromberg, J.C. 1998. Functional equivalency of saltcedar (Tamarix chinensis) and Fremont cottonwood (Populus fremontii) along a free-flowing river. Wetlands. 18: 675–686.

U.S. Department of Agriculture (USDA), Animal and Plant Health Inspection Service (APHIS). 1999. Wild pigs: hidden danger for farmers and hunters. Agricultural Information Bulletin. 620: 3–7.

12. Forest Health Condition

Purpose

This indicator addresses forest mortality impacts to hydrologic and soil function due to major invasive and native forest pest, insect, and disease outbreaks and air pollution.

Condition Rating Rule Set

12. Forest Health Condition Indicator	A small amount of the forested land in the watershed is anticipated to experience or is experiencing tree mortality from insects and disease and from air pollution.	A moderate amount of the forested land in the watershed is anticipated to or is experiencing tree mortality from insects and disease and from air pollution.	A large amount of the forested land in the watershed is anticipated to or is experiencing tree mortality from insects and disease and from air pollution.
Attributes	**Good (1) Functioning Properly**	**Fair (2) Functioning at Risk**	**Poor (3) Impaired Function**
Insects and disease	Less than 20 percent of the forested land in the watershed is at imminent risk of abnormally high levels of tree mortality (a level of 25 percent in a stand is deemed to represent an uncommon, rather extraordinarily high amount of mortality) because of insects and disease.	Between 20 and 40 percent of the forested land in the watershed is at imminent risk of abnormally high levels of tree mortality (a level of 25 percent is deemed to represent an uncommon, rather extraordinarily high amount of mortality) because of insects and disease.	More than 40 percent of the forested land in the watershed is at imminent risk of abnormally high levels of tree mortality (a level of 25 percent is deemed to represent an uncommon, rather extraordinarily high amount of mortality) because of insects and disease.
Ozone	Ozone causes a decrease in biomass growth in fewer than 20 percent of the years evaluated.	Ozone causes a decrease in biomass growth in 20 to 40 percent of the years evaluated.	Ozone causes a decrease in biomass growth in more than 40 percent of the years evaluated, and/or the watershed is within an area exceeding the National Ambient Air Quality Standards for ground-level ozone.

Additional Guidance

1. Insects and disease. Once outbreaks occur, we can do very little to halt or slow the spread, thus in this condition classification, we treat the presence of imminent outbreaks as if the undesirable condition already exists.

2. Insects and disease. Forests will use the 2006 National Insect and Disease Risk Map (NIDRM) (Krist et al. 2007) as a beginning point for evaluating potential future conditions. Areas at risk on NIDRM represent locations at which current stand or ecological conditions indicate that potential exists for insect and disease activity in the near term (i.e., next 15 years) if remediation is not undertaken. NIDRM is an integration of 188 individual risk models constructed within a common framework that is adaptable to regional variations in current and future forest health. The 2006 risk assessment introduced a consistent, repeatable, transparent process from which spatial and temporal risk assessments were at various scales. Primary contributors to the risk of mortality included mountain pine beetle, oak decline on red oaks, southern pine beetle, root diseases, gypsy moth, pine engraver beetle, fir engraver beetle, Douglas-fir beetle, spruce beetle, hardwood decline, and western pine beetle. The threshold for mapping risk is the following: the expectation that, without remediation, 25 percent or more of the standing live basal area on trees greater than 1 inch in diameter will die over the next 15 years because of insects and diseases. Krist et al. (2007) mapped watersheds most at risk at the 4th-level HUC (see fig. 11) showing the percentage of forested lands at risk. The lowest risk category (0–20 percent) is assigned as Condition Rating 1, the 20 to 40 percent category is assigned as Condition Rating 2, and more than 40 percent is assigned as Condition Rating 3. These breakpoints are consistent with recent investigations of watershed impacts following mountain pine beetle outbreak in Fraser Experimental Forest in Colorado (Rhoades et al. 2008).

3. Insects and disease. Finer scale maps at the 6th-level HUCs are available from the Forest Health Technology Enterprise Team (FHTET) in Fort Collins, CO.

4. Insect and disease detection surveys. Aerial sketch mapping is the primary data-collection method for this annual dataset. Observers code polygon data with damage agent, damage type, and a range of other possible attributes including host, severity, and approximate dead trees per acre. Data describing the condition within the polygon can be continuous or discontinuous and serves mostly as a snapshot in time of current and past activity. These data are subjective in nature, but may add valuable information for watershed assessment, particularly in areas where large mortality or defoliation events have occurred. Information about Forest Service Insect and Disease Detection Surveys are available from http://www.fs.fed.us/foresthealth/technology/adsm.shtml. Contact the local Forest Health Specialist for assistance with assessment of current insect or disease outbreaks.

5. Ozone. Assessments should use data from a nearby ambient ozone monitor or the national GIS coverage based on the ozone monitoring network. The attribute rating is determined by the percentage of years during which modeling shows that biomass growth is reduced by 10 percent or more. Contact the local Air Specialist or Forest Health Specialist for assistance with this analysis.

6. Ozone. Any years where the soil moisture is low (i.e., during a drought), the watershed(s) should be classified as "Good" because it is unlikely the ozone exposures contributed to any biomass reductions.

7. Ozone. The forests are encouraged to obtain ozone bioindicator data from the national Forest Health Monitoring program or by conducting field surveys if a watershed is consistently being rated as poor. The presence of ozone symptoms on ozone-sensitive species indicates a physiological response to the chronic or acute ozone exposure.

Rationale for Indicator

Healthy forests are an important component of watershed health. Two primary influences on forest health are insects and disease, and air pollution. Insects and disease along with fire are important regulators of forest change. Insects and disease can negatively affect resource values and ecosystem functions including reducing the ability of forest canopies to intercept snow and prevent excessive runoff. Recent increases in insect outbreaks have created a resurgence of interest in their effects on water quantity, water quality, and increased fire risks. Relatively few studies have examined the hydrologic response of forests to insects and disease, especially at long-term scales

or in large watersheds (WSTB 2008). Although we still have much to understand, we can extrapolate the effects of insects and disease on watershed condition from general principles derived from studies of timber harvest and fire (MacDonald and Stednick 2003). Investigations of a recent outbreak of mountain pine beetle (*Dendroctonus ponderosae*) in Fraser Experimental Forest in Colorado indicate that spring and fall nitrate concentrations were 30 percent higher during 6 years following onset of bark beetle activity than preoutbreak concentrations (Rhoades et al. 2009). Air pollution effects are addressed by the effect of ground-level ozoné on forest vegetation. Ozone can cause reductions in photosynthesis, which can decrease the amount of root growth, tree height, and crown width, which makes the weakened trees more susceptible to insect attacks (Lefohn 1992, Lefohn and Runeckles 1987).

Indicator References

Krist, F.J., Jr.; Sapio, F.J.; Tkacz, B.M. 2007. Mapping risk from forest insects and diseases. FHTET 2007-06. Washington DC: U.S. Department of Agriculture, Forest Service, Forest Health Protection, Forest Health Technology Enterprise Team. http://www.fs.fed.us/foresthealth/technology/nidrm.shtml. (August 2007).

Lefohn, A.S. 1992. Ozone standards and their relevance for protecting vegetation. In: Lehohn, A.S., ed. Surface-level ozone exposure and their effects on vegetation. Chelsea, MI: Lewis Publishers: 325–359.

Lefohn, A.S.; Runeckles, V.C. 1987. Establishing a standard to protect vegetation—ozone exposure/dose considerations. Atmospheric Environment. 21: 561–568.

MacDonald, L.H.; Stednick, J.D. 2003. Forests and water: a state-of-the-art review for Colorado. Colorado Water Resources Research Institute Rpt. No. 196. Denver, CO: Colorado Water Resources Research Institute.

Rhoades, C.; Elder, K.; Hubbard, R.; Dixon, M. 2008. Streamwater nitrogen during mountain pine beetle infestation of subalpine watersheds at the U.S. Forest Service, Fraser Experimental Forest. Poster presented at American Geophysical Union, fall meeting 2008. http://www.fs.fed.us/rm/boise/AWAE/scientists/profiles/Rhoades/AGU_FEF_MPB_final.pdf. (24 March 2011).

Water Science and Technology Board (WSTB). 2008. Hydrologic effects of a changing forest landscape. Washington, DC: National Academies Press, Committee on Hydrologic Impacts of Forest Management. http://www.nap.edu/openbook.php?record_id=12223&page=R1. (24 March 2011).